Prepublication kudos for DAD AND SON by Art Klein

"Fascinating . . . a voyage on discovery of oneself . . . beautifully written."
—T. Berry Brazelton, M.D.

"I love this book. What a refreshing read! A funny, sad and delightfully candid memoir that not only rings true for every parent, but is a wonderful story to read and savor."
—Margery D. Rosen
Family and Childcare Editor
Ladies' Home Journal

"*Dad and Son* is wonderful! It is rare to read so psychologically and emotionally satisfying a book—and come away happier, stronger, and enriched both as a father and as a son."
—Justin Frank, M.D., President
Physicians for Social Responsibility
Professor of Psychiatry
Georgetown University Medical Center

"This is a superb book! A wonderful story about loving and growing and fatherhood."
—Karl Horwitz, President International
The New York Times Syndication Sales Corp.

"Art Klein emboldens us about men's feelings the way Atlas once lifted the world to retrieve our buried joy and pain. Mr. Klein's honesty and caring embrace our hearts."
—Simon Perchik, Poet

"It reads like a thriller—a compassionate thriller about fatherhood. I loved it!"
—Carey Winfrey, Editor
American Health Magazine

"*Dad and Son* made me reflect on what it's like to be a man: definitely not the day at the beach I somehow assumed it was going to be. Art Klein has done us all a service and I thank him."
—Tom Paxton, Folksinger

"Moving and wonderfully well written . . . a fascinating examination of what it means to struggle as a man today."
—Shawn Coyne, Associate Editor
Bantam Doubleday Dell

"Wonderfully written and full of all the right feelings and emotions. It made me feel guilty that I'm not spending enough time with my kids, which is a positive comment about the book."
—Bob Bender, Vice President, Trade Division
Simon & Schuster

"*Dad and Son* is a gift to us all. From the heart of your masculinity, I felt embraced. Your book stands as a testament to what it means to be a man."
—James Sniechowski, Ph.D, Founder and Director
The Menswork Center

"Must reading for all parents and would-be parents—whether male or female. I was riveted! *Dad and Son* is bold/tender, raw/caring, sweet/hellish, very funny, compelling and totally human."

—Judith Sherven, Ph.D, Clinical Psychologist and
Gender Reconciliation Authority

"Magnificent! Art Klein captures the magic in the parent/child relationship and shares that magic with his readers, through tears, laughter and growth. A must read."

—Brook Noel, Editor/Publisher
Single Parenting in The Nineties

"Have you ever felt like you were taking on the whole world? What if you could not get out of bed or lift up your son to give him a hug? Men will see hope in their own tragedies when they read this book. I highly recommend *Dad and Son*. It is emotionally charged with something that our society says does not exist—the inner feelings of a man."

—Kevin Sheahan, President
Greater Pittsburgh Chapter
National Congress for Fathers and Children

"A book fathers will treasure forever. The most honest account I've ever read of a father and his kids. It should be required reading for every new dad."

—Peter Baylies, Publisher
At-Home Dad

"Your book is too filled with wit, wisdom, world-weariness and wacky wonderfulness not to be read by every parent in America. It could be THE primer for the men's movement."

—Robert Sides, Founder
The Massachusetts Men's Political Caucus
Director, The Men's Internetwork (TMI)

"I found myself drawn into it. It is a wonderful book. An important contribution to the literature about fatherhood. I hope that both new and experienced fathers will read it."

—Stephen Harris, Editor and Publisher
Full-Time Dads

"Congratulations on an outstanding contribution. This is an excellent, powerful, insightful book that explores what being male is all about. It speaks to me about my own relationship with my father and my sons and my role as a male in America."

—Peter M. Lisi, Superintendent of Schools
Pocantico Hills, New York

"A wonderful story with personal and universal insights for all men."

—Robert Ware, Founder
Men International
Melbourne, Australia

DAD AND SON

DAD AND SON

A Memoir About Reclaiming Fatherhood and Manhood

Art Klein

TORTOISE BOOKS

AN IMPRINT OF OCTAVIA PRESS
CLEVELAND, OHIO

Printed in the United States of America
Pagemaking and design by Kathleen Mills
Cover design by Bill Szilagyi

Library of Congress Catalogue Card Number: 95-061622
ISBN 0-940601-10-9 (Hardcover)
ISBN 0-940601-11-7 (Softcover)

For additional copies, call or write:

Individuals and Organizations   *Trade*
Tortoise Books   Octavia Press
191 Harbor Watch Court   12127 Sperry Road
Sag Harbor, New York 11963   Chesterland, Ohio 44026
516-725-9465   216-729-3252

DEDICATED TO

My daughter Zoe,
for her love and understanding

Robby Stein, who encouraged
me to write this book

Carlton H. Thiele, in memorium

Instinctively, as do the shipwrecked, he will look around for something to which to cling, and that tragic, ruthless glance, absolutely sincere because it is a question of his salvation, will cause him to bring order into the chaos of his life.

— Soren Kierkegaard

CONTENTS

RAISING MY SON

JOURNEY TO RAISING A SON

I had been bedridden for nearly four years with a life-threatening neuro-muscular disorder when my son Isaac was born in May of 1984.

I had thought all of my adult life about having children. Holding a baby in my arms was a thrill as far back as I can remember. The idea of having children of my own made me feel I could be a man who could love. That still sounds odd to me. For reasons I'll never understand, though, that's what I wanted to be from the time I was an adolescent. Even in grade school, I can remember imagining what it would be like to be a father. And realizing I probably would embarrass myself if I shared this idea with my friends.

Now I felt devastated.

I had made it through the worst of my illness. But I was still in nearly intolerable pain and mostly incapacitated—unable to be out of bed for more than a half an hour at a time. I had no reason to think I ever would become well enough to raise myself, no less Isaac. I had missed out on much of the first three years of my daughter Zoe's life; she had lived daily with the horror of my seemingly imminent death. I no longer believed I could parent. I no longer knew if I believed in a life worth the pain. My mind felt in a shambles, clattering terrifyingly about years lost, about having to start over again, including fighting my way through a lifetime of concerns and anxieties about being male.

I didn't think I could do it.

And I wasn't sure I wanted to try.

That was then. Today, nearly a decade later, I mostly have recovered from my illness. I have two children I treasure. I have an abundance of

---

love and friendship in my life. I often feel blessed to be alive. It all feels miraculous to me. It *is* miraculous.

When I first began working on this book, I focused on the crippling deformity of my illness and my rage about it. My writing went nowhere. I seemed to do little more than learn how to artfully create the sense of silent screams on typed pages.

About a year later, though, with my condition continuing to improve, I found myself more and more wanting to write about my experiences with Isaac. Our dad/son relationship. Our hugs and giggles and talks and tears. Our times together. Our love.

Somewhere, during the nightmare years of being terribly sick—losing the power of movement, sight, sound and clarity—I felt I had died and had to start over, or go away. I wasn't sure which path to follow until Isaac was born. Until his maleness touched so relevantly on my heart and struggles.

I *would* have to begin anew. Retrace the crawling stuff little boys do—touching and cuddling, being spontaneous and playful, being howlingly honest. I would have to rethink more grownup things—from being a dad to reevaluating the hunting I used to enjoy, from trying to understand why I never had allowed many men to get close to me to defining and believing in my own courage. There was no choice but to try again to see my way through this whole confusing and unlearned business of being male.

After alternately ignoring and kissing Isaac for the first two weeks of his life, I knew that, in order to go on, I had to risk loving him with all the life I had in me. Some of my recollections of these times make up the first eleven chapters of this book. The writing fed me. I laughed and cried while I wrote. I sometimes felt so emotionally exhausted from a sentence, from a single idea, I had to lie down for an hour and think about whether what I was saying made any sense at all.

I completed most of this writing—two years of note-taking and two years of writing drafts—when Isaac was between the ages of two and five. Then, when the book was about to go to press, I felt the need to update thoughts and feelings about myself and Isaac by adding a "Further Reflections" section to the end of each chapter.

After completing the initial drafts of these first chapters, I was able to go back and take another look at my years of incapacitation. But in a different light this time—trying to make sense of how the process of deterioration and recovery had changed me and reshaped my thinking about being a father and a son, about being male, about raising myself again as a man.

It was especially important to me that I recall the terrifying years of having been so physically weakened I couldn't lift my newborn daughter or son. Because it was precisely when I lacked the props that often define maleness and fatherhood—an assured physical presence and a thriving career, for instance—that I was forced to think about what if anything *did* define me. My powers of recall and the anguish that teased my memories just out of reach deadlocked for months. But finally there were some answers.

Men are supposed to have answers, of course. And, until age forty, I thought I did have them. My life as a male had seemed fairly typical. I had played sports as a kid, dated, gone to college, launched a corporate career, married, started my own business, divorced and remarried. Then, abruptly, *nothing* about my life was typical. In 1980, at age forty, I developed severe difficulty walking. Six months later I was bedridden. Three months after that, my wife, Dava Sobel, and I had our first child, Zoe.

This book doesn't tell you as much about Dava as it might. Our marriage ended in divorce and in a decision to share the care of our two children. Dava deserves her privacy. Beyond that, most of the experiences I write about occurred when she was away on writing assignments. That's when being a dad, and seeing how well I could manage on my own, were most intensely felt.

I also am limiting what I write about Zoe. There are reasons for this beyond the obvious one of my writing about dad/son feelings. Zoe will be fourteen when this book is published. She, too, deserves her privacy.

Still, I cannot bring myself to wind down this introduction without telling you *something* of Zoe. She and I have a special closeness—an embrace born of life-and-death concerns, a zany humor which unexpectedly and simultaneously overtakes us. Zoe has an uncannily developed ability to read between the lines of people's expressions and words; we talk a lot about her observations. She is, I should add, though you may have already guessed it, remarkably intelligent and creative. She also is beautiful. In many ways, she knows me better than anyone else does.

DAD AND SON

When I was at my worst, then later recovering from my illness, Zoe gave me the love I thought at first I didn't deserve. The love I needed for sustenance. The love I needed to become Isaac's father. I dedicate this book most of all to her, the baby I had longed for, the daughter who helped me to reach the feelings I needed, to *know* I could get well.

I feel better now about closing this introduction . . .

During the first three years of being bedridden, I had neither a diagnosis nor a prognosis. I continued to write and earn a living, and function in other ways, but in an increasingly numbed and terrified and insular manner. Normally, when people are ill, even if it's "just" a matter of having to spend a week in bed with a bad flu, they tend to get irritable, then start to "lose it." In more ways than I knew, I *had* lost it. Every aspect of my being male, every badge worn on a jutted chest, every bravura layer of posturing, every mask and wall, every contrivance and dissemblance, all these things came apart.

The questions I once didn't think about became the breaths I took.

What traits in a man make a father a good father? Do I have these traits? Fatherhood aside, is there a point to whatever else I do with my life that has anything to do with my being male?

How am I like and unlike other men? I often don't know where to put my doubts. Where do other men put theirs? And how do they keep from being consumed by them?

Can my children love me even though I am handicapped? Can I love myself? Are a father's physical handicaps harder or easier for a child to put up with than a father's emotional handicaps?

What is it like to love a son? To be loved by a father?

Would I ever feel like a man again? And what would that *mean*?

And how do I see my own father now?

It's been several lifetimes of odyssey, this illness and recovery, these thoughts about being male and raising a son and raising myself.

When I began writing this book, I couldn't run or climb steep hills or walk in my bare feet or sit through all-day meetings. I still can't as well as I would like. I needed hand controls to drive. I was in pain nearly all the time.

But compared to the years when I couldn't sit at all or stand for more than ten minutes at a time because of the rare myopathic disorder I suffered from . . . when I struggled to make a living as a bedridden freelance writer in spite of being unable to use a pen or pencil for very long or do any typing . . . when I spent two years inventing a way to be able to drive a truck standing up in the hope that I might someday be able to drive myself to business meetings . . . when I became legally blind almost over-night because of massive cataracts caused by my illness . . . when I had no one to talk to about how frightened I was . . .

Compared to those times, I'm thriving. I feel thrilled and indescribably fortunate to be alive and well and writing this book.

I write it, as writers do, to try to recall and understand. To collect small truths. To gather smiles and tears as remembrances. To burnish my children's love and life spirits in my heart. And, if I get lucky and write well enough, to pass on a few threads of the material of our common humanity.

I write out of a lifetime of contradictory doubt and certainty about being male.

I write out of a new sense of life I never expected to have.

I write, most of all, because I want to put an arm around you, the reader, and feel a kinship, and try to let you know something of what this journey has felt like to me.

IS SEX ORANGE OR LEMON?

"Would you be embarrassed if your booby showed in public?" Isaac wanted to know.

He was snuggled down next to me in the middle of an elegant, bedspread-covered queen-size bed at the Beekman Hotel, the end of the first day of our first trip.

The day had gone well. On a quiet summer weekend in Manhattan, with our search for parking made easier by a special permit for the handicapped, we had found a curbside space for my new vehicle just a block away from the hotel. I was driving a 1987 GMC step van, blue, 19 feet long, $9\frac{1}{2}$ feet high. It had been three years in the planning and modifying, and this was only the second time I was driving it by myself to Manhattan. No one knew for sure, but the best guess from the transportation experts in Washington and Albany I had worked with was that the vehicle was probably the only truck in the world that allowed its driver to either sit or stand and drive with hand controls.

Isaac liked our smartly renovated weekend-rate hotel suite, especially the television and phone in both the bedroom and the living room. We had just returned from seeing *The Little Mermaid* at a movie theater with fantastic popcorn, and had even gotten Isaac to and from the bathroom twice without missing much of the movie or losing our seats.

I had just read the last of Isaac's three favorite bedtime books, *Beanie* by Don Freeman, when Isaac reached his hand into my shirt, rested it on my chest and popped his question about my booby showing in public.

"Men usually don't get embarrassed about their nipples showing in public," I tried to reassure him.

IS SEX ORANGE OR LEMON?

"Yes, but suppose a woman with a baby walked up to you on the street and saw that you were a nice man and asked you to hold the baby and then the baby said ga ga goo goo and opened your shirt so people could see your booby?"

I tried to picture an attractive woman and baby approaching me on Fifth Avenue during a pell-mell lunch hour to scrutinize my booby. I couldn't imagine it. I had no idea what Isaac was thinking. "It would be okay if a baby did it. I wouldn't mind," I told Isaac.

"But what if the baby wanted to suck on your you know what, the thing on bottles?" He knew the word.

"Nipple?"

"Yeah, what if the baby wanted to do that?"

"Babies can get milk only from a woman's breasts," I pointed out, wondering how he was feeling about being away from his mom.

He stared at the ceiling for a moment. "Dad, do you have to do the penis/vagina thing with a lady to have a baby?" I lay there quietly for a moment, feeling as if he had changed the subject yet hadn't, as when a dream segues into a new setting with new characters, but without altering the basic mood of the dream.

"Yes, you have to do that to have a baby. But only when you want to and only when you're older." It was actually a relief that this was the topic Isaac had brought up on our first trip together. *Any* topic other than worrying about my physical condition and ability to take care of him on this trip was a gift to me.

The penis/vagina thing had been a popular phrase around our home recently. A few months ago, Isaac's older sister, Zoe, age eight, had wanted to know more about how babies were made. The answer she had gotten from her mother and me in the past about people in love lying closely together was now too vague for her. So we told Zoe the facts. And now, either because Zoe is a naturally gifted teacher or because we had answered her questions too explicitly at the dinner table, Isaac knew.

And because Isaac knew, and enjoyed nothing more in life than sharing discoveries with classmates, his entire kindergarten class was at risk of taking incalculable leaps forward in sex education.

The risk soon became reality. A few weeks after our dinnertime discussion, I overheard him explaining the mechanics of sex to a playmate after school. After making up an impromptu skit, and assigning himself

---

the role of enlightened father explaining a delicate subject to his son, Isaac wrapped up his stick-it-here-and-there monologue by saying, "No doubt you'll think the penis/vagina thing is disgusting at your age, Son." You could all but hear the rimshot when he added the closer, "But that's real life for you."

"Sounds fine to me," his friend had replied. I said a little prayer that the friend's parents would find comfort in their five-year-old son having such a good attitude about sexual intercourse.

Isaac's kindergarten teacher-aide also was privy to Isaac's latest ruminations. While preparing for Open House Night, she had asked the class to verbalize and illustrate several ways of completing the statement to parents: "I love you . . ." One of Isaac's answers had been "I love you for making me." The aide, perhaps wondering what kind of illustration might accompany the phrase, asked Isaac what the words meant to him. Isaac said he couldn't tell her; his dad didn't want him talking about it in school. She took him aside—her curiosity having gotten the better of her—and now she, too, knew.

Isaac got into his pajamas and began testing the trampoline quality of the hotel mattress. I stood watching him, amazed as I always am by his beauty, his startlingly good looks, his loving nature, his being. I don't really believe what I tell him about how babies are made, because I can't fathom that I or anyone else has the power to create life. I don't know how or why we get here.

I did clearly remember Isaac's birth, though. My fears about being able to raise a boy had been so great, it was a relief to actually see him for the first time. I almost had forgotten that boys start out as babies, not as Pop Warner linemen.

Isaac had kicked Dava into a state of unexpected gasps for months. Now he gave one final flurry and fairly whooshed himself into the world sixteen minutes after we reached the hospital's labor room. (I had called an ambulance for Dava; a moonlighting chauffeur I had kept on call took me.) Dava was still dressed in a silk blouse and one shoe when Isaac was born. Fortunately, the doctor's catching ability was better than his gestation calculations. He had declared that morning—probably loud enough for Isaac to hear—that Isaac would be ready in two weeks. Given my son's penchant for playing the rascal, it was the ideal comedic setup.

Isaac was perfectly shaped. He looked as beautiful as all creation. He lay in his mom's arms and searched her face, murmuring all the while. He had wriggled violently for months. Now he added sounds to this momentum, soft-pitched melodic hums that made it feel as if he were the comforting one. The nurses stayed on to watch him. I know that newborns can't smile, but, believe me, Isaac did.

Giggling with delight now, Isaac leaped higher and higher on the hotel bed. He landed on one foot and scrutinized me closely. "Dad, what does it feel like when your seeds go down your penis?" he asked. "Is it like mud?"

Maybe I could get him to talk about gardening. The two of us had talked recently about what kinds of vegetable seeds we would plant in our backyard garden this spring and how water would go up the roots to nourish the plants.

I explained in my best imitation of a Ph.D. type that sperm was a whitish liquid, not like mud. And that it didn't go down, it came out. And that it wouldn't be made inside his body until he was about twelve or thirteen.

Isaac suddenly looked exhausted, like he wished he had ended the night with Beanie the Bear. "Dad, just tell me what sex feels like, okay, and then let's stop talking about it."

What does it feel like? Utterly glorious when the emotions are there, when you feel close to someone you love. But what could I say that would make sense to Isaac? I had no idea. My question was: What ever happened to the kinds of questions I used to worry about my kids asking me? Like, *why is the sky blue, Dad?* I don't know, Son, it has something to do with how light is reflected, but science was never my strong suit. Pause for feelings of inadequacy. Let's look it up in your *Child's First Library of Learning.* Or, better yet, ask your science-writer mother.

It didn't occur to me at the moment that Isaac might simply want to be assured that the man's part of making a baby wasn't painful or frightening.

What to say? I had published several articles on human sexuality over the years, and still had no idea. "You know how it feels when you get stiff?"

"What does stiff mean?" He *knew*.

"Hard."

"*What* is hard?"

DAD AND SON

The subject was getting the better of both of us. Then I found myself worrying—a crazy worry, I knew—that Isaac had something wrong with him and couldn't get erections and didn't know what they felt like. I remembered the first time I saw him with one—it had startled me. But I could think only of one other time since. I asked my wife about it the next night and learned that Isaac did get erections often. One less worry.

"By hard I mean when your penis gets hard."

Isaac's lust for a definitive answer took over. "Dad, just tell me what sex is like, okay? Is it hot or cold? Or is it orange or lemon? That's all I want to know."

I put my hands over my face and closed my eyes. I was exhausted, out of answers and experiencing increasingly painful cramping, from my shoulders through my ribs and abdomen and hips, down to the arches of my feet.

Isaac tapped me. "Dad?"

"I was thinking about how to answer your question, Isaac."

Hmm. Let me think. *Orange or lemon?*

"It doesn't feel like hot or cold or orange or lemon, Isaac. It doesn't feel like anything in your life I can think of, and you're too young to be thinking much about it, but I can tell you this. It's possible at times for this whole sex and love thing to make you feel like you're floating, flying so high above clouds that you travel to a world even more beautiful and peaceful than ours, singing a song so joyous and compelling that everyone wants to stop and join you."

He looked totally confused. He *was* totally confused. Why couldn't I explain more clearly what lovemaking felt like? What *did* it feel like? I couldn't even figure out how or when to quit.

"You know how wonderful you feel after a great night's sleep?" I tried again.

"Yeah."

"Well, now picture that feeling *plus* being really excited about something."

He lit up. "I felt really excited this morning about making this trip with you."

"Uh huh." Well, maybe that made some sense. Or, maybe Isaac's question contained the answer. Why *couldn't* sex be like orange? A nice color, close enough to red to symbolize passion and love.

IS SEX ORANGE OR LEMON?

"Is it better than a trip to Disney World?" he asked.

"Yes. It's the most enjoyable sensation you can think of."

"I don't want to talk about this anymore," he said.

"Me either," I said. "We've talked about it enough for now. Let's get back to it in about ten years."

Isaac started leaping high on the mattress again. Then stopped. "Dad, I think sex sounds like green slime lime. Kind of disgusting. I'll probably adopt babies."

Lime, huh? Could well be. Could even well be I was making my way toward being a decent dad.

The world was filled with wondrous possibilities.

FURTHER REFLECTIONS

The first trip to Manhattan with Isaac filled me with more overwhelming feelings—it was more exhilarating and scary—than any moment in my life since Isaac's birth.

I had worked two to three hours every day for nine years to function well enough to make this trip. I'm certain I'll never again feel so urgent a need to perform well at anything.

Until now, when I had wanted to take my children more than thirty minutes from home, I had needed to hire a driver and try to seem like the parent in charge of their lives while lying on a mattress in the back of my own van.

Now I was in Manhattan with Isaac, with strains of "New York, New York . . . If you can make it there . . ." resounding in my cells, it seemed. I felt as if a new life for me could be conceived in hope.

I was actually taking my son on a trip.

On the worrisome side, Isaac would be seeing things about me I had kept from him until now. I would have to take several rest breaks while driving. I would need to go back to our room between excursions around the city to ease my cramping muscles. He would see me resting and icing and using medication throughout the day and night.

Stuck on the physical, and concerned whether Isaac would think of me as a cripple—as less of a dad than he had imagined—I almost forgot that the point of the trip was simply being with Isaac. He and I were good at just being with each other, too. But my larger experience was still more than forty years of being uneasy with, often intimidated by, males. No question—thinking about physical problems was easier.

As we walked into the hotel lobby, I recalled how my dad and I had never talked about ourselves when I was little. Isaac and I talked all the time. But this was away from home. This was different. What do you say to a little kid? What would we discuss, alone together in a room at night?

I knew only that Isaac—or, perhaps, the sense of this son I felt a son to at times—would blink his sonar into the darkness my life had been. And I could only hope I had gathered enough of myself these past few years for him and me to find someone comforting and good there.

At one point in the room, after Isaac had gone on at some length about the incredible things you could find in the street gutters of Manhattan—especially treasures, garbage, homeless people and dogs—he took a deep breath and started asking me questions about sex.

When he got to "Is sex orange or lemon?" I adjusted my hearing aid and asked him to repeat the question. It continued to be, "Is sex orange or lemon?" No matter. At that instant, the question could just as well have been "What's under the carpeting in this room, Dad?" or "How much love can arms hold?"

All questions seemed irrelevant to me at that hour, a late hour that felt more like morning waiting to be born—all except one question that had been galvanizing me and bearing down on me for five years: Could I be there for my son and help raise him?

And a final part of the question: Could I, somehow, someday—I had no idea how—take in through breaths of love from this boy what was worthy and decent and contributing in males, and learn how to raise myself?

BECOMING A DAD

Isaac got off to a shaky start this morning, the first morning of his mom's three-week trip.

Usually he starts the day by bounding down the steps, lurching to a halt two leaps from the bottom, wedging his face against the railing—framing the rails in his smile and honey-blond curls—and yelling good morning to me in a way that uplifts me more than a personal fitness trainer ever could.

Today he walked down the steps and murmured a quiet hello. No, he didn't want his favorite breakfast of scrambled eggs and cheese, just cold cereal.

After a spoonful, he said he had a stomachache. He didn't feel like eating. I felt my forehead, then his. Then I felt his arm just in case his head had fooled me. He felt cool. I got out the thermometer anyway and handed it to him. He put it under his tongue and sat docilely. He didn't even try to test his strength by snapping the thermometer in half as he had done a few weeks ago.

I told him his temperature was normal. He told me his stomach hurt more now. I asked some questions, the real point of which was to create an impression that I knew what I was doing.

"Where is the pain?"

He pointed to his stomach.

"Is it a sharp pain?"

"No."

"A dull pain?"

DAD AND SON

"Yes."

"Are you nauseous?"

"A little."

He had a stomachache. My own stomach began to grumble. I was recovered enough from my own long illness to drive the kids to a doctor if necessary. But sometimes I still got frightened and nearly overwhelmed if they became sick. I still tilted in battle at the one absolute certainty about kids and sickness and life in general—I just didn't have enough answers and, to reach shore safely every time out, I was going to have to be blessed or lucky or both.

"Dad," Zoe brought me back to the problem at hand.

"Yes, sweetheart."

"I want to get to school early and buy books from the Book Fair."

"I'm sorry, Zoe. Isaac has a stomachache. I have to deal with that first."

Zoe grimaced. It wasn't fair, she said.

It was very fair, I rejoindered.

Not, she said.

"If it were *your* stomach that hurt, you'd want me to take care of it, wouldn't you?" Good point, I thought. Not the greatest tone, though.

Zoe put her hands on her hips. *Female Oppressed by Male* read the caption on the classic painting in my mind. She was eight years old and I was expecting her to be the helpful wife, grown up and understanding. It *wasn't* fair.

"I'm sorry about the Book Fair, Zoe. I really am. But it runs for a couple of days. I promise to get you there the minute school opens tomorrow morning."

"They'll be out of the books I want by tomorrow."

I considered screaming. Isaac beat me to this level of emotive theatrics by emitting a small moan, a sound that asked whether I had forgotten about him. I had. I turned back to Zoe. "I'm not discussing this with you anymore now. When you're sick I worry about you. Isaac is sick now and I'm going to take care of him. And that's that."

"Okay," Zoe said. Isaac moaned again. I had to hand it to him. He moaned better than most kids.

Zoe came over to my chair and whispered to me that Isaac probably wasn't sick, but maybe he missed Mommy and needed a day off. I

---

whispered back that she was no doubt right. I kissed her. If we hurried, I told her, we might still be able to get her to school in time for her to buy books.

"You're getting the day off," I told Isaac. "And we're getting you to school at the speed of light," I told Zoe. I handed both of them their jackets and walked out the back door. They followed me. We got into the truck. I started the engine and turned to look at them. It dawned on me that, in real life, you *can't* leave a house with kids as fast as I just did. Something must be amiss. I scrutinized them closely. Zoe had her backpack and lunch. Isaac was wearing pants. His fly was closed. His fly was actually *closed*. We might never do as well again.

After we dropped off Zoe at school, I set up Isaac with a small mattress, a quilt and two pillows on the kitchen floor in front of the television. I put a drink of apple juice within his reach, explaining that his favorite, orange juice, might make his stomach worse, and told him I would be writing in my office until lunchtime. After lunch I would read him his new Time-Life book about insects and take him to the local mall to rent him a video. "I think your stomach is nervous about Mom being away and that you need a break from school," I said. "I'm sure you'll be fine tomorrow." He nodded.

I worked on a brochure for an educational publisher for fifty minutes before I couldn't stand the thought of Isaac's being alone. I walked the short distance from my office to the kitchen, put my exercise mat next to his mattress and watched a cartoon show with him for a while. He was quiet and snuggly.

At noon I offered him chicken-and-noodle soup, figuring it was the perfect food because it allowed him to feel sick while still enjoying something that he liked to eat. He demurred, explaining that he had been looking forward all morning to eating whatever I had packed in his lunchbox the night before.

I was surprised. You can't feign a stomachache while eating a bologna sandwich. Besides, when I was a kid—I love that phrase even though (or because) my kids go bonkers when I use it—I got hot meals from my school cafeteria. Ever since then I have always felt sorry for kids who had to eat from a lunchbox.

Lunchboxes should be banned. They're unseemly, bordering on obscene. Excess jam oozes out of peanut butter and jelly sandwiches.

DAD AND SON

Mustard cakes the lunchbox latch. Crumbs you missed with your kitchen-counter sponge beg for carbon dating. Lukewarm juice packs leak. Bologna sandwiches go bad. Carrots go limp. And Teenage Mutant Ninja Turtles pictured on the outside lose the Ptomaine War with The Great Mutant Mold inside.

Isaac apparently didn't buy my lunchbox theory. Exuberantly, as if Christmas and Hanukkah were merging at this instant, he flipped open his self-contained adventure complete with the treat of his choosing lying in wait.

He smiled beatifically at what he saw. His expression said: My next life should be half this good. He said, "What are *you* eating for lunch, Dad?"

"Peanut butter and jelly." It seemed appropriately empathetic. Also, I almost had forgotten how much I loved peanut butter (crunchy style) and jelly (raspberry jam, with big seeds, so that you get double the crunch).

"Want some of my bologna sandwich?" he asked. "It tastes great with lettuce and American cheese. Thanks for making it my favorite way, Dad."

I was happy he didn't seem sick anymore.

"I'm glad you like it," I said. "I'll try a bite." It *was* well-nigh perfect. Enough mustard to cake a lunchbox. Enough air in the white bread to absorb the rest.

"Dad?"

"Yes."

"I want to be a builder when I grow up."

"That's nice." The peanut butter was making it hard for me to talk. "You'd make a good builder."

My father (one of the world's great nonbuilders), I recalled, used to hit his fingers more times than he did nails and my concerned mom was always trying to hide his hammer. In the eighth grade, I had scored in the bottom eleventh percentile of the nation in a spatial relations test.

"You'd make a great builder," I told Isaac, hoping that my hammer-weak genes would skip a generation.

"I'd build you a tree house, Dad. Would you like that?" I considered grabbing him away from his lunchbox and hugging his mustardy body.

"I'd love it." What a kid. A few hours ago, he couldn't cope with going to school. I give him a few moments of my time. He takes care of himself most of the morning and now he feels good enough to be a dad himself.

BECOMING A DAD

We started talking about a mockingbird that had lighted on the far railing of our back deck, then went on to other things before I went back into my office. But the next day after school, Isaac seemed to pick up the boy-as-dad thread of our discussion.

"Dad, if I had a baby boy someday, how would I keep him from swallowing a marble and killing himself?"

"No problem," I said. "Don't have any marbles around." Zoe would have found this mildly funny, or at least recognized it as the kind of awful joke I love to tell. Isaac, at age five, was often too earnest and literal to respond to my verbal silliness. He preferred kinetic and visual humor— being tickled, pretending to trip and fall, hiding in a garbage bag, attaching a quarter with bubble gum to his thigh and saying it was a tattoo.

"I was joking, Isaac. Seriously, you're asking me if you could keep your own child safe, right?"

"Right."

"You definitely could. You'll be great at it."

"But what if I forgot something dangerous and the baby died?" I reminded myself to not forget anything that might be dangerous to Isaac.

"You already know a lot about keeping babies safe," I said. "You would keep sharp stuff in drawers, have childproof lids on medicines, things like that."

He looked frightened. "Maybe I shouldn't have a baby. I wouldn't like him to die. Could I just rent one to play with at your house?"

I got up and lifted him out of his chair and sat down with him on my lap. "Isaac, I promise to keep you safe. And, no, you shouldn't rent babies. When you're older and married you should have your own babies. They'll be very lucky to have you for a dad."

"I know one thing about babies, Dad."

"What's that?"

"I'll hug my baby a lot to make sure he knows I love him."

"I like that," I said. A part of me, however, a diminishing part that I increasingly wanted to kill off, fretted about Isaac's being too kind. I recalled being told by several people close to me when I was about to graduate from college that I was too nice to go into business; I would be devoured. Tender, kind, nice, nurturing. I still had trouble accepting those "womanly" characteristics of mine.

That night, after school, I took Zoe and Isaac to our one local fast-food restaurant. The two of them invented games while we waited for our food. I initiated what would become a tradition for us: Guess when the food we ordered would be announced over the loudspeaker; the one with the closest guess wins a quarter. I won, but the kids enjoyed the contest and got the quarters anyway. I sang made-up nonsense songs to them on the way home. Then we all sang along at the top of our lungs to our then-favorite traveling song, Barbara Cook's rendition of "Sweet Georgia Brown."

At bedtime, Isaac said he felt fine about school tomorrow. I gave him a goodnight hug and started to say my "prayers" to him while lying next to him, the same incantation he had recited to me every night for the past two years: "Goodnight, sleep tight, sweet dreams, don't let the bedbugs bite, I love you, I'll see you in the morning."

I got no further than "goodnight" when Isaac interrupted me. "Don't say your prayers yet, Dad. I wasn't ready for you to stop hugging me."

I knew it was true the instant he said it, as if I had always known it about myself. I toyed with the idea that I merely had been in a hurry to spend time with Zoe and then get downstairs to my office. But that wasn't it. The fact is I had gotten uncomfortable hugging this male child of mine.

"Thank you for telling me that, Isaac." I lay down next to him and gathered him close.

With his face buried in my chest, I allowed myself a few tears. One rolled off my cheek and settled, like an unbroken raindrop, on a cowlick of Isaac's springy curls. I thanked him silently for helping me learn how to be his father.

FURTHER REFLECTIONS

"Want to see something really amazing?" a man asked me.

What with the clamor and clinking of a wedding party going on around us, and the man talking into my left ear—which had gone ninety percent deaf when I was ill and stayed that way—I thought he had asked me if I wanted to *see someone really angry.*

I *did* want to. I don't like parties. I had been smiling vacuously at anyone and everyone and agreeing to god knows what. Seeing someone angry would be more fun than my bobbing around like one of Geppetto's charges.

BECOMING A DAD

I looked toward the masses of people at the catered affair, waiting for my new acquaintance, Paul, to show me that really angry person. Paul tapped me on the shoulder. I was looking in the wrong direction. "Out there," he said, pointing toward two little kids playing catch with a football.

Wonderful, I thought. The guy's got better vision than me, too. "Isn't that amazing?" he exclaimed.

It might have been amazing. Only I had no notion what *kind* of amazing it was.

"My son is the one catching the ball now," Paul guided me in a slower and louder manner.

"Amazing," I said about the routine catch. Paul stared at me as if I were retarded. "It isn't the catch that's amazing." he said even more slowly, moving closer to me, speaking directly into my hearing aid instead of looking at me, making me yearn for one of those old ear trumpets that at least keep people yelling at a respectable distance. "It's what you're about to see now. *In fact, right now!*"

I widened my eyes and gave him what I imagined to be a thoroughly dazzled, truly amazed look. His kid passed the ball to the other kid. "Did you see that?" he fairly ejaculated.

"Sure did," I said. *See what?* I wondered to myself.

"Thirty-five yards on the fly. *Wham*, right into that kid's chest. Right between the fucking numbers. Perfect spiral. *Zap*. A fucking blind man could have caught it." I wasn't so sure about that. "*Right into his motherfucking chest for christsakes*," Paul explained.

"And here's the good part," Paul went on. "We're talking only nine."

"Nine," I repeated with gusto. Nine fucking *what*, I wondered.

"Nine fucking years old," Paul replied, as if uncannily reading my thoughts.

The kid, not the ball, I knew. "Incredible arm for nine," I said.

"Are you kidding?" Paul inquired. "It's [this time I was ready and joined him by lip-synching the chorus] *fucking amazing*."

I've heard stories like this one from proud dads all my life, and I understand the braggadocio BS. Pride in a son's accomplishments is there in me, too. It's the punchline to all this pride that bothers me, the resolution of it for the father going on so excitedly about his son's body parts. An arm in this case. But it could just as easily be a leg (the kid booted his first thirty-yard field goal at age ten—straight through the fucking uprights) . . . or legs (he set a high school record in the mile as a fucking sophomore) . . . or muscle power (he bench-presses twice his fucking weight after only a year of lifting) or muscular ligature (fucking washboard stomach, biceps the size of your fucking legs, legs the size of your fucking tree trunks, tree trunks the size of your fucking whatever and so on). The emotional outcome for dads of sons who perform athletic feats like these, whether spoken or not, is: "This is the thing about my son that makes me a proud father." Or, more pointedly, in the words of one man commenting about his track-star son: "When I saw him cross the finish line first and set a new record for the mile, I felt I really and truly had become a father."

Isaac isn't a superstar athlete. He has exceptional talent for writing poetry and song lyrics and stories. I'm pleased, even thrilled, that he's blessed with this ability, and I encourage him to use it. But nothing he *does* is what actually makes me proud of being his father. Nothing he *accomplishes* makes me feel "I truly have become a father."

I felt I had become Isaac's dad when *he* talked about becoming a dad. I felt I was a good father when I realized *he* wanted to become one. I realized I had done something right as a parent when I saw Isaac's interest in "fathering" kids and friends and the environment, and, in general, doing all the nurturing and protective things I believe males have a special gift for doing, if they get any encouragement at all in this direction as children.

I used to think only of the body parts involved in becoming a dad. The body parts needed for conceiving Isaac, lifting Isaac, throwing a ball to Isaac, wrestling with Isaac.

But that's not right, of course.

These body parts are mere bystanders to love. I finally have accepted the idea, after years of merely realizing it, that if I had never gotten well physically, it still would have been possible for me to become Isaac's father in every way that mattered.

My heart has to perform well. That's all that matters.

MISSING MOM

It was the fourth day of my wife's three-week book tour.

When I went into Isaac's room to wake him for breakfast and school, he sat up out of a deep sleep and immediately reminded me that sometimes it is hard for him when his mom is away because she's the one who hatched him. I gave him a hug and carried out the post-hatching chores as best I could by going downstairs to make him his favorite breakfast: scrambled eggs with melted cheese.

At bedtime I read him another chapter of *Charlotte's Web*. It was our first time reading this book, and as it turned out, our last, since the inevitability of Charlotte's death spoiled the story for Isaac. I already had read the book at least five times to Zoe, and we had found more to like and admire with each reading. As he lay there listening, Isaac sucked from his bottle of orange juice, swishing each mouthful in his cheeks for a minute or so before swallowing.

"I don't think that humans are as easy to trick as this book makes it seem," he said, referring to Charlotte's ability to spin letters in her web and inspire people to believe that the words formed had preternatural origins.

"I'm not so sure," I said. "A lot of people are willing to be fooled about things they want to think of as magical. Besides, you know, animals might be smarter than we think."

"Okay," Isaac said. "Animals might be smart, but Mommy is pretty stupid. She didn't even remember to take the hamsters' wheel out of their cage. The squeaking sounds of the wheel are going to keep me awake."

"The hamster cage is downstairs in my room," I said. "And I took the wheel out before I came up. . . . Isaac?"

DAD AND SON

"What?"

"It's okay to miss Mom."

He didn't even pause. "Do you know what they expect me to do in kindergarten?"

"What?"

"Work and learn. And not have any fun. Those people in school are trying to destroy my life."

"Did something happen in school today that made you unhappy?"

"Nothing made me happy."

I couldn't tell whether this was another disguised grievance about his mom being away. Or whether Isaac was complaining about a traditionally structured class environment where his impulses for fantasy play and reverie had few outlets and where he was expected to listen attentively to voices that weren't his own musings—something he hadn't yet learned to do very well.

"Did anything bad happen to you today?"

"No." He bent his torso in several directions at once, head pointing down off the side of the mattress, hip on his pillow, feet on my chest. "You're not listening, Dad. *Nothing* happened. It's just that they're destroying my life."

I ordered my God-why-me thought to leave. It took its time.

"Did you have any fun at all?"

"Just the teeniest, weeniest bit," he conceded.

So it wasn't the greatest day at school. Time to go to sleep.

I looked at him again. His expression now was almost identical to the look of the two newts his mom and I had bought him a few months ago, shortly after his fifth birthday. By the time we had gotten the newts home and into a fishbowl—the same bowl that just days before had been the instant deathbed of his two birthday goldfish and his two next-day replacement goldfish—they wore the clamp-mouthed, grimly satisfied expressions of people who had just beaten the deadline for signing their living wills. Their measly lips never opened, not once, not even for food or outrage. We buried them the next afternoon and not out of spite.

Thanks newts and happy birthday, Isaac. And thanks for performing your newt imitation tonight, Isaac. It's just what I needed.

Thank *you*, Dad. And thanks for this great life. Four stiff goldfish and two croaked newts for my birthday. How about an undertaker's set for my next birthday? And now Mom's away, too. Probably won't ever be back, either.

It's embarrassing to be thinking about newts when your kid needs your help, but Olympic-level diving into obsessive anger happens to be one of my specialties, and the fact is that the little bugger newts *hadn't* even had the decency to last a single night. Who knows. Maybe in their previous lives they had been owned by little boys and thus wisely had opted to throw themselves on the tiny, plastic pirate's sword Isaac had put in their bowl to keep them company. Or maybe they had held their collective newt-breath until they had turned newt-blue. In any event, so much for children being intuitively at one with all living creatures.

Isaac looked less like a newt now. "Isaac, maybe the problem at school isn't just a school problem. Maybe it's that you're not in such a good mood. Maybe you're sad about your mom being away."

He pulled away from me and began crying. "Why did she have to go for so long? Why can't she be like other mommies and take short trips? Why is everyone leaving me?"

I repeated facts about the trip in an attempt to calm him, emphasizing that his mom would be back the next evening for a weekend visit before leaving again. I wasn't leaving, except for a few hours at dinnertime tomorrow. He would be fine.

"I'll never make it," he groaned. Then he yelled, "I won't be able to make it and then what will happen to me?"

"What won't you be able to make?" I asked, my voice rising. I was starting to take this too personally. A few years ago, I hadn't been able to care for my kids at all. Now that I was able to do more, I wanted to be appreciated. Instead my kids were treating me like a normal parent. I wondered whether my years of incapacitation would ever go away for me. My recollection of it was present almost daily, a thicket underlaid with quicksand where I feared I couldn't protect myself or my kids.

I tried to hold Isaac in my arms, but he wasn't having it and thrashed away toward the wall.

"I won't be able to make the three weeks!" he yelled.

I kept trying to hold him. He finally relented. "I'm going to help you make it," I said.

"I already *know* that," he snapped.

My anger got the better of my fear. "Dammit, Isaac, let me tell you something. I'm not a goddamn magician, I'm a father. Not everything I do makes you feel better. That's the way it is, and if you don't like it, it's too bad.

"I'll always try to make you feel safe and loved, do you understand that?" My words and tone were definitely at odds.

"I feel better," he said.

I hoped so, but wondered whether he was merely being wary. His smile said otherwise. He looked very pleased. Big revelation for Dad: Isaac had needed me to tell him unconditionally to stop carrying on.

I straightened out his snarled sheet and blanket, tucked him in again and kissed him goodnight. Then I went into Zoe's room and apologized for spending so much time with Isaac. I was delighted to be with her. Our times together in the evenings were often the loveliest part of my days.

She looked angry.

I didn't want to believe that.

"What's the matter?" I asked.

"You took Isaac's side before he went to bed. He should have known better than to write on the special 'Please knock' sign I made for my door. You don't sign in on a knock sign; you sign in on the sign-in sheet."

"Zoe, I know that," I said, "but I don't think Isaac did anything bad on purpose." She glared at me. I looked at her sign and reconsidered. Isaac had scribbled all over the damn thing. Zoe had worked hard to make that sign. It meant a lot to her. So did the basket outside her door she had decorated with "U.S. Mail" and a red felt flag.

"I'm sorry, sweetheart. I didn't realize what Isaac did. I missed it. Maybe I'm a little frazzled, too." She still didn't look happy with me. "Do you want to talk more or read?" I asked.

"Read."

I lay down on her bed, opened *Then Again, Maybe I Won't*, a wonderful book by Judy Blume, and got ready to start a new chapter. Zoe rested her head on my shoulder and exhaled slowly, a signal that told me she was ready to read and talk.

Unexpectedly, sucker-punched by uninvited feelings, I felt like crying forever, for all the things I hadn't been able to do with my children, for all the joyous times that could have been and never were and never would be. I struggled for control, the open book lying on my chest.

MISSING MOM

Zoe waited a moment, then touched me gently on the cheek. "Are you sad, Dad?"

"Yes," I said, "but I'm okay."

Thinking about what the day had been like, about how I could take care of my children now, I started reading, my voice quavery with the most exhilarating feeling: These kids of mine knew me pretty well. And seemed to love me anyway.

FURTHER REFLECTIONS

Incredibly to me even now, I had been so caught up trying to comfort Isaac when he missed his mom, I forgot how much I had missed my own mom. I can't remember ever *not* having missed her when I was young.

The day after I was born, my mom's older brother told her that their mother had colon cancer. The collision of my birth and my grandmother's predicted death, as well as my mom's resultant depression and her having to care for her mother away from our home, left me shuttled around from neighbor to neighbor feeling misplaced and frightened. "You were shy and nervous then," my mom recalls.

Sometimes I felt my mom's absence most of all when she was with us. In my most traveled memory loop, starting from when I was four years old, I can picture her in bed, lying on her back, sobbing. I stood in front of her half-open bedroom door for a minute, watching and listening, calling softly to her a few times, then continued on into my sister's room. My mom cried for hours. My sister slept with me that night; I think I asked her to.

In another memory, I see my mom's youthful eyes and mouth teetering on rage or sadness, with me trying to guess which. I remember, early on and seemingly always, studying my mother's face. I still some-times read people's expressions more than I listen to their words.

My mom recently told me of my dad's reaction to those times. "After you were born, your daddy said I shouldn't have any more babies, because it made me too depressed."

I'm sure I felt I had made my mother sick. I say that, in part, because when Zoe was four, she asked me for the first time if her being born had made me ill. I tried reassuring her in different ways over the years. I think she knows now—I hope she knows—that what she did was help me get well.

I recall, as if from birth, wanting to help my mother feel as if she were not dying along with her mother. Saving lives came to dominate my personal life. Until recently, I spent most of my adult years looking for, and finding by the score, troubled people to help keep alive and well.

At age five, Isaac, of course, missed his mom when she was away. He worried about her some, too. What if she didn't come back or what if she died? I found, after weeks of trying to put his fears in perspective, that the simplest truth of all about his mother was the most calming: Your mom will be back because she loves you.

Quite a pair we were, Isaac and I. He missed his mom and I missed being well. I missed being loved in a way that seems to give some people a kind of intuitive, cradling ease with children. I missed myself, the sense of the better man I hoped I could one day be.

When I wasn't with my kids, when I wasn't being a parent, I had little idea who or what I was. I had been in three-times-a-week therapy for nearly two years. I was struggling with the worst despair I ever had felt—being elevated just enough now from the depths of my illness to have a realistic view of how sick I really had been.

My mother and sisters worried about whether I could physically manage the kids with Dava away. They offered to come out and help.

I didn't want them to come. The only way I knew how to evaluate my progress, and my prospects, was to see how good a father I could be.

That I had to see for myself.

MR. MOM AND MR. DAD

"So you're Mr. Mom these days, are you?" a woman acquaintance asked when I picked up the kids at school toward the end of their mom's three-week trip. I nodded yes.

"How does it feel to be Mr. Mom?" another woman asked me as we were walking into the supermarket. It was apparently her way of saying hello, because she walked away before I could answer.

"So!" another woman burbled as we were loading a ton of groceries into the truck and I was trying to finesse Isaac's mourning a piece of candy that he had just dropped. "*Now* you know what we go through all the time, *Mr.* Mom, isn't *that* right?"

Right. I mean, wrong. That is, look lady, scat with your clichéd concoction of Michael Keaton in *Mr. Mom* and Dagwood Bumstead as Quintessentially Bumbling Dad. I help raise kids, dry tears, fold laundry and whatever. Off my case, please.

"Yeah, I know what you go through," I told my latest interrogator, impressed at how thoroughly her smiling face contradicted her undertone of vindication and not just a touch of smugness. "I love taking care of my kids," I said, closing the truck door on her irksome presence.

Zoe giggled. "I don't think that lady was too happy with you, Dad."

"Yeah," Isaac added. "But she probably doesn't juggle oranges in the supermarket, so she may not enjoy shopping with kids as much as you do."

I do usually get a kick out of doing mundane stuff with Zoe and Isaac, even though I'm the same person who loathes the notion of shopping for anything, except by mail. I enjoy being with my kids. I enjoy, rage, laugh, fume, sing, muse, and sometimes wish the two of them would get out of my sight and leave me alone. But I'm mostly delighted by their presence. Having children is what I wanted. I didn't have any in my first marriage. It looked like I would be too ill to be an active parent in my second. So, yeah, you bet I love being Zoe and Isaac's dad.

That's not to say I would survive if I had to limit my days to vacuuming and shopping. But I look forward to the hours I spend every day with my kids and, for that matter, with as many of their friends as they want to invite over.

Besides, the odiousness of typical mom chores is as much myth as reality. Going to the supermarket hardly has to turn into hegemonic violence. ("Ask for candy one more time and I'll smack your little head in." I've heard that punchline and its more abusive variations ever since I was a kid; it's downright scary.) Shopping can be shared time. Fun time. And I say that even though I have a reaction to shopping that literally makes me feel crawly, itchy and on the brink of losing all rational thought after twenty minutes. So, when my wife is away, the kids and I *have* to make shopping fun, or not eat.

Wannabe professional athlete that I was, I'm still big on imaginary world speed records. The kids and I time our food shopping. I assign missions and goals. Dangle bribes. Dash around offering encouragement like a basketball coach ensuring that set plays happen by running up and down the sidelines barking out directives.

Zoe, get any three fruits you want. Or, get three kinds of fruit even if you don't want them. Isaac, get any breakfast cereal that's more nutritious than the box it comes in. Both of you—do this and that and more before the count of fifty and we'll meet at the bagged-candy shelves and get some of that bad stuff. To keep up the highest levels of motivation (and, more or less incidentally, to mortify the kids), I often hustle after them juggling oranges or announcing into a cucumber their incredible shopping feats.

In any event, misery isn't shopping after a hard day's work. It isn't cooking or mopping up or wiping a messy tush. Misery is having a sick child you can't help. It's being sick yourself and *not* being able to shop, cook and bathe your kid. So, yeah, lady in the parking lot, I *do* know something of what you go through taking care of children. And I think it's great that you do it. And I think you're luckier than you know.

The fact is that, sibling bickering aside, the only thing that's not much fun about being "Mr. Mom" is being called "Mr. Mom." The phrase is inane, since it implies that dads can't take care of kids unless they transform themselves into male versions of moms. (No doubt the reason moms are never called "Ms. Dad" is because no one is quite sure what, if anything, dads do with or for children.)

Anyway, the role of Mr. Mom is comparatively easy for me. It's being "Mr. Dad" that takes more thought.

The daunting if clichéd question—*am I man enough?*—has nagged at me from the start. I was always uneasy about the horseplay, the hi-how-are-you punching and shove-you-for-proof-of-virility scuffling that many boys seem to take to naturally. I was a popular kid. But scared of most everything and everyone.

My dad was never like that, not nervous the way I was, not that I knew of back then. He had been a star athlete in college. He was the highly respected superintendent of schools and preeminent civic leader in our small town. His den and office spilled over with trophies and awards. When the Lions Club added to his collection by naming him Man of the Year, former Hit Parade pop singer Bea Wayne sang "Mr. Wonderful" to him on the stage of the school auditorium. Dad was a hard act to follow. As I grew up, with my doubts about masculinity growing with me, my dad's acquaintances would often stop me on the street and say in cheerful voices, "Lou Klein's son, are you? Well, son, let me tell you something: If you become half the man your father is, you'll do very well for yourself."

That was the problem. I felt like half the man my father was. I felt stuck. If I grew to be like my dad, there would be approval (from my dad). If I went with my more inward-looking nature, I might not get approval. Worse, I wouldn't know *who* I was. I didn't know anyone like me.

But here we are now. And damn if I don't feel reasonably good about myself—at least some of the time. Still sensitive (as in "Please understand that Arthur is a very sensitive child"). Still empathetic (as in "I can talk to Artie about my problems"). Still oohing and aahing at babies (as in "Some boys don't like to babysit, but Artie doesn't mind; he takes naturally to babies"). I used to hate those traits of mine. Hate myself for having them. They were soft traits, I (and seemingly everyone else) thought more for girls than for boys.

I thought wrong.

DAD AND SON

I am sensitive and caring. Most men are . . . especially with their children . . . most especially, where the so-called tough guys are concerned, when no one is looking. There's no need for the stereotypically silly label, "Mr. Mom." A dad being just as able as a mom to parent. Just as able to love.

The role of a dad is indefinable only to adults. Kids know what dads are. And kids know they need them.

Isaac underscored this point tonight by asking me at bedtime about stepchildren. What did it mean to have a stepbrother or stepsister? And would he ever have one?

I gave him an example. If his mom married another man, and that man already had a son and daughter when she married him, the son would be his stepbrother and the daughter would be his stepsister. Zoe's, too.

"Of course, I don't mean that your mom *is* marrying someone else," I hastened to explain. "You understand that, don't you?" Great example I had given him. "Mom went on a trip because she has to work."

"I'm not worried about your getting divorced if that's what you're thinking," Isaac said. "The problem is that Mommy is going to miss Halloween."

"She isn't," I corrected. He was totally discombobulated about time.

"She is, I know she is," he said bitterly. "My favorite day of the whole year, of my whole life, is going to be ruined because of Mommy."

"Isaac, look at me. Read my lips. Repeat these words after me. *Mommy . . .*"

He decided to go along with this President Bush lip-reading game.

"Mommy."

"*Is.*"

"Is."

"*Going.*"

"Going."

"*To be here Halloween because she loves you, loves Zoe, loves me, loves Halloween and would rather be a roasted Halloweenie than miss that day with you.*"

"I can't say all that, weenie brain," he replied.

"Never mind saying it, can you remember the point? That your mom will be with you on Halloween?"

"Yes." He looked contrite.

By the next day the subject of stepsiblings had tumbled around more in Isaac's mind, the mind that seemed to sprout new brain cells and synaptic connections every hour.

"Dad," he said during our bedtime snuggle.

"Yes, Isaac."

"Why don't you and Mommy get it over with and one of you get me a stepparent. One of you isn't enough, you know."

"I know," I said. "But your mom is on a business . . ."

"Dad, I know what she's on. And I don't want to hurt your feelings, but you're not Mom. And that's that. So how about getting me a new mom or bringing back the old one?"

"Mommy will be back to spend the weekend with you and Zoe. You don't need a new mommy, you need to get some sleep. Okay?"

"Okay, but I don't like it."

"Sorry, it's the best I can do."

"Dad?"

"What?"

"I'm sorry if I hurt your feelings. You're not doing a bad job."

"Thanks, Isaac. And, don't worry, you haven't hurt my feelings. For some reason I feel good. I feel good about just about everything except that you miss Mom. But that's okay, too, because your mom will be back."

About a year later, Zoe and I were routinely cleaning out candy wrappers, parts of board games and bits of jewelry from her clothing drawers in order to make room for clean laundry. She discovered a beautifully decorated note in her sock drawer. "Isaac and I made this for you when Mom was on that long trip," she said. "We meant to give it to you."

The front of the card had a big "Thank you!!" embellished with clusters of carefully drawn purple balloons. Inside was a glued-on sticker showing a smiling ambulatory tomato holding more balloons. The words next to the tomato, in Zoe's writing, said:

DAD AND SON

Dear Dad,
Thank you for being
such a good father and
mother.
Love,
Isaac and Zoe

I thanked her. She grabbed the note from me to read it again. "I didn't really mean that you're a good mom, but that you're a good parent. But don't let it go to your head, Dad."

I assured her I wouldn't. I saved the note. Mr. Dad was not likely to get overconfident.

FURTHER REFLECTIONS

Men who hate women are *misogynists*.

There is no equivalent traditional word for women who hate men.

Men who help raise children are jokingly referred to by women as *Mr. Mom*.

There is no equivalent phrase for working women who raise children. They're not *Mrs. Dad*. If a man jokingly refers to a woman as *Mrs. Dad*, he minimally will be condemned as a politically incorrect lout.

If a heterosexual man is a good father, he still has to be concerned about whether he is a "real man."

There is no equivalent struggle for straight women. If they are good moms, they are real women.

There are more than a few recent books, *The Courage to Raise Good Men* being one of them, as well as scores of articles, assuring women how well they can do raising sons by themselves. Fathers, no less father figures, aren't needed, we're told. A woman can initiate a boy into manhood without a man around.

There are no equivalent books and articles for single dads raising daughters. Fortunately. Because this currently faddish only-one-parent-is-needed theory has little to do with human beings except in the abstract. The reality is that boys need good men around and girls need good women around. Kids *can* do without one or the other. But ask them—they'd rather not!

MR. MOM AND MR. DAD

Dads used to be defined as men who slept with moms, pitched in with conception, brought home the bacon, mowed the lawn and did fix-it chores around the house. If they helped raise the kids, it was barely acknowledged, scarcely respected. Moms raised the kids. Dads did other things. And that was that.

Today, when some thirty million men function either as full-blown parents or have jobs that emphasize caregiving, no one knows quite what to make of them.

There is a virulent bias against men as caregivers. We're leery about entrusting our young children to them. For example, we are neither irked nor up in arms over the reality that elementary school children don't have many male teachers. Turn this picture around: If there were nine male K-3 teachers for every woman, it would be a burning national issue. Justifiably, too.

We take pains to revise our history textbooks with pointed examples of courageous and achieving women who were more than just moms. Or not moms at all.

We take no pains, we give no thought, to revising our textbooks with examples of courageous and achieving men who were good dads. The very idea sounds silly. It isn't silly though—it's desperately needed if boys and girls are to break through the destructive myths about themselves and about each other.

There is a "mom, flag and apple pie."

There is no equivalent American paean that includes dad.

I'm not Mr. Mom or Mr. Dad or Mrs. Dad or any such thing. I'm one of millions of men, with the number growing, who has forsaken power in the workplace to be an active parent.

I'm a father. It's what I've always wanted to be. It's what I almost always love doing. It is the only thing in my life that day in and out makes me feel like a good man. A real man. A man.

No need for applause. Lots of need for less ridicule.

YELLING AT ISAAC

I yell at Isaac more than at Zoe.

It's not that Isaac is bad or does bad things. It's just that there are times I only have the patience to deal with a boy rather than with a spontaneous buzzsaw.

To notice Isaac is to love him—and, just a matter of time—to yell at him. After three days of kindergarten, his teacher termed him a pip, his teaching aide called him (with her eyes rolling) an irrepressible cutup, his principal characterized him, *sotto voce*, as a pisser, albeit a very special and endearing pisser. He was and still is all these things. He also is dimple-cheeked, curly-haired and engaging. Intuitively decent and relentlessly generous. Madcap and philosophical. Captivating, sweet and snuggly. Sensitive about human behavior. A tad shy of medium-sized. Impressively intelligent. And noticeably handsome.

In addition, he is a person who can insinuate himself into my life more good-naturedly, enthusiastically, lovingly—and maddeningly—than any other human being of any size I've ever met. Our battles are different from mine with Zoe. Not just because of the kids' different personalities, but because of the male-to-male dynamics involved, no matter that I scarcely understand these dynamics.

Knock, knock . . .

I pay no attention because I'm in my office. And, because before I went into my office, I had made absolutely, positively certain that Isaac had everything he needed—including orange juice, a big hug and an upcoming hour of Batman on TV—in order to comfortably leave me alone while I worked.

YELLING AT ISAAC

I stare at the computer screen for half an hour. At long last, the idea that I'm struggling with starts to surface. Knock, knock again. Isaac surfaces first. And launches full throttle before I can protest. "Hi, Dad, excuse me, I know I said I wouldn't bother you, but I was pretending the kitchen chair was a monster going to destroy the world, so I tied it to the door going down to the playroom and now I can't get the knots undone and I have to get down there right away and rescue . . ."

I yell at him.

Unlike with Zoe, who suffered along with my illness for five years, it's a giddy relief for me, a normal parental pleasure, to yell at Isaac. I yell at him. My wife yells at him. His teachers yell at him. Zoe yells at him. Rarely his teenage girl baby-sitters, though. It's hard for them to yell at someone they wish were old enough for them to date.

Isaac doesn't listen well—that's mostly it. Of course, when his kindergarten teacher says so, I resent her lack of patience. What's *her* problem, I wonder? Doesn't she realize he may be thinking about something more important than "Mr. M stands for munchy mouth?"

On the other hand, if Isaac doesn't listen to *me*, let's say because he happens to be holding conversations with extraterrestrial gods about how to save humankind from itself, it's another matter. I yell at him.

Put Isaac in front of a television and he's a deaf turnip, even with the set *off*. Blotto. My father reincarnated. "Isaac," I say. "*Isaac*." "ISAAC, I'm talking to you." "*ISAAC!!!!*"

A tiny, otherworldly voice, "Yes, Dad."

I want to say: *Isaac, dammit, I've been yelling my ass off at you trying to get your attention, what the hell is the matter with you?*

What I actually say: "Would you like some juice before I go into my office?" My voice as small as his. It's my small, controlled voice, the one strangled by puzzlement about why I ever wanted to be a parent if I object so vehemently to being disregarded.

Sometimes I rant and rave because I'm in physical pain and have to lie down for a while fairly packed in ice and specially made back-sized bags of frozen gel. Or because I feel lousy about myself and not up to being Isaac's father. When that happens, I usually feel the kid deserves better.

On the other hand, sometimes the kid deserves the trouble he gets.

One day, when Isaac was three, he went on a mischief rampage designed—intentionally, I felt—to surpass the limits of my sanity. It wasn't just this one day, of course. He had been working up to the confrontation for a few months. I can't remember all the things he did within a few hours that day—but some highlights were determining whether one of our cat's eyes would come out, giving Zoe an experimental, short right to the solar plexus and swinging his toys like wrecking balls at the living room lamps.

I do, however, very clearly remember the climactic event.

It was a warm summer night. My wife and I were in the kitchen, wishing that half an hour more would pass so Isaac could be put to bed. Isaac was on the deck outside the kitchen. I yelled to him to stop playing with the garden hose and turn off the faucet. He didn't stop; he watered the gas grill. I yelled again. He watered the cats. I bellowed for all I was worth. He opened the slider door leading into the kitchen and with a stick-it-in-your-ear leer said, "What, Dad?" I again calmly shrieked that he should put the hose down, realizing only blurrily that he was still holding aforesaid hose. He suggested that the kitchen floor needed cleaning. And pulled the nozzle trigger. And swamped the kitchen floor.

I leaped up as if shot, whacked him once on his butt, yanked him up to his room and slammed the door, shrieking the obligatory inanity: When you learn to be a civilized human being you can come out and join us.

He remembers the event to this day, three years later. Daddy, still somewhat shaky physically, was finally something of an authority figure. Using even the gentlest physical force to effect civility is brutish, at least according to a theory espoused by Art Klein before he had children of his own. But maybe once or twice in a lifetime it can have a good outcome. It has worked that way for me.

Mostly, my yelling at Isaac is about things that Isaac can't believe any fair and decent person would yell about.

He stands on his chair during dinner, tilts the chair back and comes perilously close to slamming his head through the glass doors of the pine hutch behind him. I yell. He accuses me of caring more about the pine hutch.

He ties a rope between two objects on either side of a room and I trip over the rope. I yell. He says he wants to be a magician who does rope tricks and at least he's not just wasting his life watching television.

He sneaks up on me when I'm wearing my hearing aid and pretends to be the world's loudest ambulance siren. I yell. He says it's not his fault he was born with a loud voice.

YELLING AT ISAAC

He covers the kitchen floor with grape juice. My feet stick to it. I'm irate. Irate? I'm *pissed*.

"Damn it, Isaac, you poured juice all over the floor again."

He looks offended.

I feel unsure of myself. His mom and I routinely ask him to pour juice for himself, except if he has to work with a full two-quart bottle. The full two-quart bottle has tempted him.

Of course, I can be easily offended and highly self-righteous myself. The kid has learned from the master. I say nothing more for as long as I can hold out. About a minute.

I use my contrite voice to say that I don't like to yell, but I have asked him millions of times to not pour the unopened two-quart bottle of grape juice, and that if he feels he must disobey me, to at least not continue trying to fill a small juice glass with it until most of the juice in the big bottle is on the table and floor, is that clear?

He glares at me. I take offense at his glare because it denies all understanding of what I'm saying and all aspects of being sorry.

I also feel bad for him. He tries so hard. And I'm wildly proud of him for all the things he's learned to do. Then there's this to consider: God help me, but it has to be one exquisitely fine sensation for a four-year-old child—or anyone, really—to dump most of a two-quart bottle of grape juice on a kitchen floor.

Isaac watches my face carefully. Then suggests I think he is a bad person.

I say maybe I overreacted, and didn't mean to imply that he was a bad person, and don't think so, and, in fact, love him even when I'm yelling at him.

He isn't appeased.

I suggest that he is a good person, a *very* good person, in fact, a wonderful little boy who just wanted to pour juice by himself.

"And it's important to learn to do new things, isn't it, Dad?"

"Yes, Isaac, it is."

The following week, when he accidentally poured grape juice on the kitchen table and floor, I told him I thought he had done well to keep some of the juice in the bottle.

DAD AND SON

FURTHER REFLECTIONS

At the time Isaac was born, I had never in my life yelled at a young child. Not my peers when I was a kid. Not Zoe.

I wanted to be like my father. My father had never yelled at me.

When I was twelve, I asked him, admiringly, how he managed to avoid losing his temper. He told me he used to get explosively angry. Then, one day, when he was in his early twenties, before he married my mother, he blew up at someone in a way that made him feel disgraced. He vowed he would get rid of his temper; he would never yell again. He never did—at least not at me.

I wish he had yelled at me. I would have felt more recognized by him—the loudly acknowledged pain in the ass a child is entitled to be at times.

At his extreme, my father would express his dissatisfaction with me by slightly amplifying his tone of lecture. I think this more blunted approach is scarier to a kid than being yelled at (my mom *did* yell at me), because you don't have a decibel meter to gauge just how much trouble you're in.

The loudest my dad got with me followed several similar incidents within a few months, when I was taken out of my second-grade classroom for "fiddling with myself" and sent to the school nurse. I must have been a virtuoso fiddler. Else my teacher and the school nurse wouldn't have risked telling my dad, the school superintendent, about a matter that was all but unmentionable back then.

Immediately following what turned out to be the last of these incidents, the school nurse told me she was going to have a long talk with my father. After school that day, I cried hysterically in my room for hours, waiting for my father to get home.

When my father entered my room, I thought he was going to hit me (even though he never had), so I kept my bed between us to protect myself. He neither yelled nor struck. He attempted to redress the problem by explaining to me that I must have an itch. And that I therefore must powder my testicles daily. That would relieve the problem, he said. Daily powdering was important.

It didn't take me long to act differently with Isaac. When he was thirteen months old, he used to crawl up to unsuspecting family members and guests and bite their ankles. After a month of this, and after my calmly and repeatedly telling him *no* and explaining reasonably that he shouldn't bite people, and after he had drawn blood from my ankle one morning, I screamed at him. I felt monsterish about this until I gradually learned from just about every parent in the world that they yelled at their kids, too.

There must be something inherently wonderful about yelling—at least that's my rationale for continuing to yell at Isaac. Kids are intuitively smart and they will yell almost all the time if you let them. I'm not sure what the magic is—getting attention, improving circulation, releasing bad feelings, forestalling angst, putting your yin and yang in balance—it must be *something* good.

Still and all, I think I should yell less at Isaac. I'm cranky by nature. And he by nature turns my crank. Perhaps I should yell more at myself. When no one is around, of course.

What I might yell:

I'M NOT THE WORLD'S WORST HUMAN BEING I THINK I AM WHEN I YELL A LOT.

YELLING CAN BE USEFUL—LIKE THE TIME I SAW ISAAC TRYING TO STICK HIS TONGUE INTO AN ELECTRICAL OUTLET AT AGE FIFTEEN MONTHS.

PARENTS MUST YELL AT TIMES IN ORDER TO RETAIN WHAT IS LEFT OF THEIR SANITY. I'M A PARENT. I MUST YELL.

NO ONE HEARS ME IF I YELL TOO OFTEN.

I SOUND TOO SURE OF MYSELF WHEN I YELL. NOT SO. I'M NEVER TOO SURE OF MYSELF.

HAVING LOST TEN YEARS OF MY LIFE TO ILLNESS AND RECOVERY, I NOW FEEL OBLIGED TO GO AFTER LIFE AS LOUDLY AS I CAN.

I HAVE NEVER YELLED TO MY CHILDREN THAT I DIDN'T LOVE THEM. THERE ARE MODEST LIMITS OF DECENCY TO MY YELLING.

I SHOULD YELL LESS, THOUGH.

I hereby promise to yell less at Isaac in the future.

STICK IT UP AMERICA, PISQUIT

Observe the furtive flasher in Times Square, whipping open his raincoat as you stroll past, exposing nobody-knows-whose watches pinned to the lining. "Psst, want to buy one?"

Parents and grandparents remind me of this kind of character when, unasked, they pull out a photo archive of kids faster than a flasher can flash. Or they pour forth a litany of astonishing and incredible things their kids or grandchildren have said.

Some captive recipients of this show-and-tell may pay attention because they think it will buy them favors at the Heavenly Gates. Others because they can't think fast enough. Still others because no matter how sentimental or silly the photo or anecdote, they know that even a brief exposure to kids makes them feel better.

Put me into this final sucker category. Sure I'll look at photos of your kids. Even if the child I'm looking at appears to be wearing a fake nose and fangs, but unfortunately isn't, I'll find something appealing, something alive and genuine, about his looks. As for hearing about what kids say, I'm all ears. Kids' voices are invariably more interesting than adults'—wonder and spontaneity not yet having been deadened.

What I treasure most about my own son's quotable expressions is not so much his winsome jabberwocky or malapropisms, although the sheer joy these give me is undeniable, but his indefatigable efforts to form and articulate thoughts about life.

He wonders a lot about how we got here and the point of our lives. Which gets me trying to rethink ageless and universal questions—the purpose of my own life, the existence of God, the meaning of being human, and the seeming inability of our species to do something as basic to sustaining life as loving one's neighbor. I find myself reformulating everything *except* the life-defining value of having kids around.

These ideas that matter, the ones that stick with you till the end if you don't go numb first, are like the thousand-piece puzzles adults and kids like to play with; you spend a lot of time assembling them, only to eventually take them apart and try again.

Of course, some puzzles are just for fun.

For example, when Isaac was three and a half, he asked my wife and me what "Stick it up America, pisquit" meant.

It was gobbledygook to us, but Zoe figured it out. In a TV movie she and Isaac had just been watching, one character had said to the other, "You're stinking up America, pigskin head." Isaac's rendition of it, "You're sticking it up America, pisquit," won our hearts. My full nickname for Isaac soon afterward became Pisquit J. Tittleberry, *tittleberry* being a word Isaac had coined just weeks before to describe what it feels like to be in love.

Philosophy is unavoidable child's play, the mind overflowing with an infinite assortment of modular and nonmodular toys until and unless someone says you've outgrown them. Tinkering with life's mysteries certainly comes easily to Isaac. (If it turns out that sewing while philoso-phizing also comes easily to him, then one genetic linkage for both will have been identified; my mom's father was a tailor who spent most of his working hours debating the manifold and often paradoxical laws of the Torah with his scholarly cronies.)

A philosopher can lend us hope that each peculiar model of life has all life at its core; that each of us is mostly, but not entirely, isolated from the other. When Isaac was three, and goaded his mom into blowing up at him in the car, he told her later, "You got so mad it was like you were all blood; we both were like blood." Anger expressed, feelings acknowledged, isolism denied, universality engaged—we go on.

A few months later, Isaac tried out another idea: "A person and a bug are the same except they don't look the same."

Isaac brims with questions that he poses and then tries to answer for himself.

Why would God create a world where people were always killing something or someone? Isaac once broke down and wept, thinking about such an idea. "If we have to murder plants and animals every day to eat, and we don't even think about it, what kind of a life is this?" he asked me.

Why would a child miss his mom more than his dad when mom is away? "It's because you mostly miss the one who warms your eggs."

On that subject, Isaac was trying to figure out why some people are nice, others rotten. "The bad ones had mothers who had rotten eggs," he explained.

What does it feel like to be in your mommy's tummy? Whenever Isaac used to reminisce about this subject, he would look especially radiant. "I wish I were there now," he would say with the special grin of delight reserved for this topic. "Everyone probably wishes it, because everyone likes a warm and snuggly place."

Why am I, his dad and a white man, not guilty of killing Indians? Because, according to Isaac, I'm tan, not white. "And a good thing," Isaac said. "Because if you had my whiteness you'd be ugly." Somewhere in our family tree there might have been someone as direct as Isaac, but no one knows who it might have been.

Seemingly mundane matters are worth considering, too. "I wonder why God invented embarrassment," Isaac was heard musing. "Maybe to see what kinds of bathing suits we would invent."

Another time we were reading about Hugh Pine, a cranky porcupine who couldn't tolerate the demands on his life made by other woodland creatures. His friend, Mr. McTosh, took pity on him and rowed him out to a private island where he could be alone. The tranquility was fine for a time, but then Hugh became morose.

I interrupted the reading of the story. My doing this usually annoys Isaac, but I sometimes can't help myself; I'm curious to know what he's thinking. "What lesson do you think Hugh has learned?" I asked.

"That life isn't perfect, I guess," Isaac answered.

I felt sad that this idea had grabbed hold of him at age five and probably never would let go. The next night he repeated in another context that life wasn't perfect. I asked him why he thought so. "Because too many people push and shove," he replied.

A week before his sixth birthday, Isaac and I were talking at bedtime about the trip I would be making to New York City to see his ailing godfather, Uncle Carl. Isaac was upset at the thought of never seeing Carl again "except when he is dead and in his casket and can't talk to me anymore."

I assured him that Uncle Carl loved him. Isaac continued to look upset, so I reminded him that although Uncle Carl was dying, which was terribly upsetting, I wasn't. I was fine. I wasn't sick anymore. Isaac remained quiet for a moment in his favorite contemplative position, lying on his back, staring at the ceiling.

"How do you start a new family, Dad?"

"You know," I said. "A man and a woman get married and they have babies."

"I don't mean that. I mean a whole family with godfathers, grandfathers, grandmothers, aunts, uncles and everything else."

"They come along with you when you get married."

"No, I mean how do you start a *human* family? I mean, you can't exactly load up a bunch of people on a dump truck and drop them off on a planet, can you?" His speech had speeded up and taken on the exasperated tone he uses when he suspects I'm going to give him an "I don't know" or "There are different schools of thought about that" answer.

I talked about how some people think that God created Adam and Eve and the rest of us, while other people think we evolved from mammals like gorillas. I also told him that although most Americans were religious and believed in God, they didn't want their kids' schoolbooks to say that God created us. I didn't understand why this was so. Nor was I at all certain about the answer to his question.

"That's okay, Dad. Don't feel bad," he said.

"God," I said silently to our possible Creator, "if you *are* the one responsible for this kid, take a bow."

"I don't think God made us; I think we come from animals," Isaac said after another contemplative dialogue with the ceiling.

I was surprised. Most of his classmates talked about God as Creator and Jesus as Savior, and until this discussion, Isaac had agreed with them.

"Why do you think we come from animals?" I asked.

"Because they're nicer than most people," he answered. "Maybe we'll get to be more like them in the future."

DAD AND SON

FURTHER REFLECTIONS

The private joke I tell myself about Isaac: He was born talking and has never stopped; he may someday pause for a breath, but if that happens, he will be simultaneously explaining how his breathing apparatus works.

People who know me casually think Isaac gets his gift of gab—or at least his penchant for going on and on, and on—from me. That may be; I often have to remind myself to give others equal time. On the other hand, it was an ordeal for me to talk during my growing-up years and well into adulthood.

When I was four, I began talking less because the fluidity of my speech had become halting, repetitive and blocked. A year later, I overheard my parents mentioning to friends that many children go through a stuttering phase and that I would no doubt come out if it soon. I knew that wouldn't happen.

When I was six, I started taking weekly speech lessons from Dr. Nellie Stevens, the drama and speech teacher at my dad's high school. Dr. Stevens had the longest false eyelashes I have ever seen and believed in equally long practice sessions. We practiced: *How now brown cow* was her favorite jaw loosener. I also worked on learning to click my tongue loudly as well as extend it out of my mouth curled.

The resuits were mixed. In the second grade, I got the role of the grandfather clock when our class sang that eponymous song. I also was the sensation of my peers for being able to make the loudest tongue-clicking sound in school.

On the negative side, my stuttering grew worse as the years passed, reaching an all-time low in the seventh grade.

That's when Dr. Nellie Stevens came back into my life. Every seventh grader had to take her speech class. I was stuttering badly in all of my classes, increasingly unable to say anything without struggling horribly—turning red, gasping for air, puffing my cheeks, twitching—the contortions of the average serious stutterer.

One fateful day, Dr. Stevens asked me to come up to the front of the classroom and recite the phrase, "Betty Botter bought a bit of bitter butter." Hard consonants were my marathon-distance wall. I never did get going. Not with the word *Betty*. Not with the stuck *B* sound. After speech class, standing on line for the cafeteria, everyone who had been in my class gathered around to ask me what the trouble was. "I don't know," I said without stuttering.

That same year, I was strongly urged by Dr. Stevens and my father to enter the school's public speaking contest. I did and spoke flawlessly, coming in a close second to Edward Minskoff's recitation of the Gettysburg Address. "Good job," the school principal said. "Tttttank yyyou," I stuttered.

On a trip upstate a few years ago, with Isaac in tow, I mumbled that I had just gone past a turn I had meant to take. Isaac took this opportunity to mention my stuttering for the first time.

"You can make great speeches, Dad" he said. "I remember your eulogy for Uncle Carl at the church. But why do you stutter sometimes when you're not making a speech?"

I don't know why. I do know that four out of five stutterers are male. And that in some tribal cultures, with clearly delineated rituals for initiating boys into manhood, no one stutters. And that it's difficult for a male stutterer to sound self-assured, confident, on top of things—manly. And that many episodic stutterers, perhaps much like food addicts who alternately binge and recant, can conceal their affliction from a lot of people.

All my life, my stuttering made me reluctant to be with other men. It was one more thing, and no minor one, that made me feel different from other men. A year ago, though, I joined a men's support group. At one point, after two of the men in the group had praised me for my eloquence, I told them I was a lifelong stutterer. However obvious my stuttering can be at times, I had never made this admission publicly. It was a relief to say it, and even allow myself to stutter on occasion at subsequent meetings. The admission to these men has helped me in other situations that typically are the hardest for stutterers—fast-food lines, telephone calls, ordering at restaurants—situations that demand speech then and there.

Outside of men's groups and other intimate circumstances, though, men are allowed to have frailties only if those frailties don't show. You can be a star athlete or business doyen, with vulnerabilities ranging from impotency to bleeding ulcers, and no one will think badly of you. Not so if you're a stutterer. Mel Tillis aside, men who stutter don't sound authoritative, in command, as men are supposed to sound.

DAD AND SON

When I was in the early stages of psychotherapy—and complaining ceaselessly and bitterly about my then-severe stuttering—my therapist asked me if I wanted to try hypnosis for it. I said no. I didn't want to let go completely of this inner cue. Stuttering is an embarrassment and a nuisance. But it's also a reminder that I'm vulnerable. That I often don't have answers. That uncertainty motivates me to write and try to make sense of my feelings. That words are seldom if ever needed to convey love. That I'm different from other men. And very much like them.

Stutter and all, these traits of mine fit into being male, a far broader category than I ever suspected, a state of mind that took me fifty years to reach and accept.

I hope it doesn't take Isaac and his friends anything near that long. They are almost eleven years old now. I overheard them talking recently about their need to feel like "one of the guys," peers of theirs who tend to be strong, fast, athletic and cool in a way that to me emphasizes remoteness.

What to say to Isaac and his non in-group friends, at least in my own mind? Practice sports more? Kick some ass? Ridicule anyone who's different? I wouldn't know what to tell them. Except for the obvious: You're good guys because you're good people.

If only it were that simple.

HOLDING IT IN

I was halfway through Isaac's bedtime story when Dava returned from a business trip. Isaac scrambled out of bed, stepping on various parts of me that had been lying next to him, and leaped into her arms.

"Can you read the rest of the Ramona chapter to me, Mom, *please*?"

Zoe wanted Dava to read to her, too. Feeling more dismissed than freed after a week of being the kids' mom and dad, I went downstairs and settled in on my office bed amid the tangle of phones, answering machines, manuscripts and coffee cups, suddenly determined to enjoy this respite I had been given and watch the Knicks-Celtics game before getting back to work.

At halftime there was a tentative knock on my door.

Before I could open it, Isaac let himself in, walked quickly by me and lay down in the cozy spot I had just vacated. He stared at the ceiling and struggled not to cry. I knelt beside him.

"Where's Mom?" I asked.

"She fell asleep with Zoe."

"What's the matter?"

No answer.

It had been a tough week. I kept one eye glued to the set. Patrick Ewing was on fire tonight. Go away, kid. "Can you tell me what's bothering you?"

He shook his head.

"I want you to be able to talk to me, Isaac. Take your time." We both glanced at the TV, which Isaac knew I never left on when I was serious about talking. John Starks sank a twenty-footer. I turned a bit more of my attention to Isaac.

He wore the expression of someone who had just been pinned to my bed by something gruesomely otherworldly, perhaps a slimy-green android equipped with malevolent coals for eyes and scissors for hands. "I'm afraid of it being like it was when I was two or three years old, when I had to get up a lot during the night to pee," he said. "Back and forth, back and forth, all night long." His upset intensified. "From the bedroom to the bathroom, from the bathroom to the bedroom, back and forth . . ." It was getting hard for him to talk and I couldn't understand the next sentence at first.

Finally his words became clear. "I'll be too exhausted from peeing to go to school tomorrow," he said. "I keep my hand on my penis all night, but I'm afraid it won't work."

"You'll get to sleep, don't worry," I said. "And you'll be fine at school, too. You've been up a lot later than this."

I realized I may not have grasped what he had just said.

"Isaac?" He continued staring at the ceiling.

"What?"

"*What* won't work if you don't keep your hand on your penis?"

The tears poured down his cheeks.

"If I don't hold my penis, I'll pee in my pajamas and wet the bed. Everything will get wet. My whole room will get soaked."

Good Lord, I thought. Go wake your mom; she's a science writer, far more knowledgeable than most people about urinary tracts. Besides, I want to watch the Knicks. They're playing well for a change. Besides that, I *had* been reading to you, fellow. *You* had wanted your mom to read.

I got up and turned off the television and exhorted myself to quit whining and grow up and be Isaac's father. I stared at him for a few seconds until I could see more clearly the little boy I loved so dearly.

I didn't know why he was so upset. Isaac was four years old now and it had been at least a year since the last time he had wet his bed.

"I want to tell you something, Isaac."

I thought momentarily about censoring myself. The thought passed. Kids are expected to say bizarre things, but I don't think their utterings approach the aberrations that clank forth regularly, if mostly unspoken, from adult circuitry, at least from this adult. That is my only explanation for what I said next.

"I've been peeing for nearly half a century, Isaac. So you can rest assured I know a lot about the subject."

That was for starters. "I've even *written* about penises," I went on. "How many dads do you know who can say that?" How many dads located even remotely close to their right minds *would* say that, I quizzed myself. And, furthermore, *were* there *ever* any other dads who had worked themselves into a situation like this? As for writing about penises, I had in fact once published a spoof in a men's magazine based on the *Reader's Digest*'s, "I Am Joe's . . .," in which I gave voice to the one part of Joe that the *Digest* hadn't permitted to speak for itself. Maybe Joe could talk to Isaac. "Hi, Isaac. I'm the authoritative talking male sex organ your dad wrote about. Perhaps he mentioned me to you. How about you and I have a little chat . . ."

More to the point, I could have told Isaac that I had once fretted about my own penis, even to the extent of going to doctors when I was sixteen to see if I measured up. The doctors didn't understand why I was worried. And, being doctors, didn't ask. My family doctor told me in confidence that mine was bigger than his. A higher-priced specialist asked me whether my erect penis was four inches or longer. When I nodded yes, he took out a speculum, inserted it into a plastic vagina, and at the four-inch mark proceeded to batter hell out of the cervix. "See what I mean," he said. I didn't, though I was fascinated. "The point," he declared, "is that at four inches you bang up against the cervix." I had the cervix confused in my mind, the mind that was busily if inefficiently constructing an anatomical map, with the clitoris. "More than four inches is wasted," he said. No one else had, or subsequently has, told me that with the same degree of conviction.

"Isaac, have you needed to pee more than usual tonight?"

"No."

"Is your penis bothering you right now?"

"No."

"Did anything happen today that worried you?"

"No."

I quit.

I didn't quit. "Let me tell you something. Every night, before I go to bed, I come up and check on you, and I have never seen you holding your penis. And I'll tell you something else . . ." He interrupted me before I could.

"I hold myself under the covers where you can't see it, Dad."

"Now we're getting somewhere," I said. "You see, I happen to know exactly what position you're in when you're sleeping. Here's the way you usually look." I got down on the floor, stretched out on my back and placed one arm over my head, the other arm near my ear.

It wasn't until later that evening that I recalled the truth: The demonstrative position on the floor was the way *Zoe* slept. Isaac slept on his side and I had no idea *where* his hands were. When he was an infant, I went into his room every night to reassure myself that he was breathing. If the reality were that he grew an extra hand every night, and held his foot with it, I would have been the last to know it.

I looked tenderly at him. He looked desperately at me.

"I squeeze my legs together when I'm not holding on with my hand. It's my legs that hold it in when my hands let go." He closed his eyes, ready, I imagined, to go to his pee-drenched death. The autopsy report: father's denseness.

"Isaac?"

"Yes."

"Isaac, we're going to talk facts now. I want you to listen carefully to me. You *are* fine and I'm going to prove it to you. I'm going to do it within the next five minutes. You're going to feel better, then I'm going to get you to bed.

"We're going to start with some really good news. Do you remember that you were one of the first boys your age to stop using diapers?"

He focused on me clearly for the first time. Either I had broken through or he was getting ready to buy anything.

"Yes. How old was I?"

"Two and a half." Actually, he was almost three. I hadn't really meant to lie.

"That means," I went on, "that you now have gone more than a thousand nights totally in charge of when you do pee and when you don't. Think about *that!* You see, you're in charge. The only way pee can come out is if *you* want it to." I would consider telling him later that kids his age sometimes have accidents.

HOLDING IT IN

"Remember the Polaroid picture I took of you when you were a tiny baby, the one where you peed right at the camera without my knowing it?"

He delighted in the memory. And told me that maybe because he was older now, he had a bigger muscle for holding pee in. I agreed, and at his initiation, we discussed where that muscle might be. Someplace "under there" was the best we could do.

"Dad, you really *didn't* know I had been peeing at the camera until after you saw the picture, right?"

"You're absolutely right." The picture was one of my favorites. Isaac had been a week old, lying in a small plastic tub of warm water, the quintessentially munchable munchkin.

He took my hand and we walked up to his room. Climbing under the covers, he wrapped both his arms around Mister Bear. I felt good that I had helped him resolve a fear. He wouldn't have to anxiously clutch himself all night long now.

I kissed him goodnight and started out the door.

"Goodnight, Dad. I'll hold myself later to keep the pee in," he said.

FURTHER REFLECTIONS

Two of the more than twenty people who read parts or all of this manuscript had a complaint that struck me as odd. Both are males and school superintendents. One was the superintendent of Isaac's school. One a retired superintendent of schools—my dad. Their complaint, phrased *precisely* the same: "There are too many penises in the book; take some out."

I joked: There can never be too many penises.

I challenged: *Where* are there too many penises? I'm writing about real life. In real life, four-year-old boys are sexual, aware of their parts, wondering about their parts, checking out, fiddling, playing, enjoying, worrying about losing their penises . . . what the hell do you want from me, it's not like I invented all this.

The reply from the superintendent of schools: We understand reality. But, we still say: Take out one or two penises. *There are too many.*

Yeah, well, we'll see. *Penis, penis, penis.* How's that? Too many? I don't think so.

53

DAD AND SON

Penis, penis, penis, penis. Too many now?

I think we should try to get past it. There's one penis on every male. Average length in, as the phrase goes, a tumescent state: six and a quarter inches. (Who did all this measuring? I don't know.) Average length in a flaccid (men hate this word) state: two to four inches. Range: one-half inch to one foot. All normal because they all exist with a number of men.

What isn't normal, or good for anyone, is the insanity about penis size. You should know this: Men stare at penises in locker rooms more than they stare at women on beaches. And . . . when men surveyed were asked whether they would rather be six-feet three-inches tall with a three-inch penis, or four-feet nine-inches tall with a nine-inch penis, sixty-four percent said they would rather be four foot nine. I swear this is true. And . . . when one thousand men were asked if they were satisfied with their penis size, one thousand out of one thousand said no.

I tell you this: If we could introduce just a tiny bit, at least one inch, say, of rationality into the subject, the world might well be at peace. Certainly, the angels would sing. Especially the male angels.

In fact, how about a chorus of angels singing on high? I've got just the right name for this song. It's, uh, oh you know.

We could call it the, uh, Blank Song.

Damn, never mind. I can't say that word.

MY PARENTS' REVENGE

My parents must have been seeking revenge last night.

Because out of nowhere it became apparent to me that I recently had been saying some of the same words and phrases to Isaac that my parents had said to me when I was little. Clichés that had struck me at the time as irritating, patronizing and repetitive. And every bit as dumb as kids intuitively know their parents to be.

The only redeeming value I could think of was that, as a kid, I had been comforted by these verbal old shoes; they were familiar cues that told me I probably would live through the crisis at hand.

I didn't reach the absolute pinnacle last night of being a ridiculous parent. But I came close enough. My mind seemed locked into a veritable treasure chest of ancient and abrasive parental clichés, which reminded me much later that evening of something quite horrible I had said to Isaac a few weeks before.

The evening started well enough. When I returned from visiting my friend Carl, who was sick with AIDS, the kids, who had been with a baby-sitter, were waiting for me on the front lawn. They raced alongside my truck as it crept up the driveway. Zoe reached me first. I picked her up and hugged her, and told her I had been to Barnes and Noble and bought her the five *Baby-sitter Club* books she wanted. She clung to me for a moment with her arms around my neck. Zoe was six years old when I could first pick her up like this, and I will always feel overwhelmed by the sweetness of the sensation and the memory.

Isaac waited patiently from ten feet away until I put Zoe down, then war-whooped and took a running leap approximately in my direction. I caught him just before he would have careened headfirst into the side mirror of the truck, nestled him to my chest and spoke into his curls while trying to memorize all over again the musty-sweet smell of them. "Hi, Pisquit, my boy. I brought you some terrific books, including a new one by Don Freeman, the guy who wrote *Beanie*. I'll read it to you tonight, okay?"

"Great, Dad. Who's Beanie?"

"Beanie the bear, you know, the windup bear who goes to a cave by himself, the book you like so much."

"Okay. Dad, I put my face into the pool today, really all the way into it, and I didn't even have to wipe my eyes with a towel right away, either."

"That's great, Isaac. I'm proud of you." I kept my grip on him as though he were a squirming newborn.

"Dad, I also got a bird whistle in a birthday grab bag."

"You got a what?"

"A bird whistle," he repeated, swooping his fist into his pocket and, without pausing, trying to blow my brains out with the object in question. When motivated, Isaac is an exceptionally coordinated child.

We went inside and said good-bye to the baby-sitter. It was late—time for wily assurances, for finding ways to say goodnight, Isaac—there will be enough love in your darkened room to still the shadows, enough light to bring the dawn.

I ushered Isaac upstairs, got pajamas out of his drawer for him and, as usual, gave him a mild overdose of instructions—don't dawdle, do brush your teeth, please get that stuff off your bed, no you can't take that toy out to play with now; I know you love it but it's bedtime. Having put the universe in order in very much the same annoying way my parents had with me, I went downstairs to check my answering machine.

A client wanted me to revise a draft of copy and fax it to her that night. Three other calls had to be returned. Just-so-very-recently loved and happy dad swore aloud, got bedtime drinks for the kids and stomped upstairs.

Isaac had made a paper airplane out of a Barnes and Noble flyer and was sailing it across the room. "Did you see that, Dad? Did you notice how it dived and almost got Charlie?"

"You could have hurt Charlie, Isaac. You shouldn't throw stuff at a parakeet; I've told you that before. Besides, what did I ask you to do before

I left your room? I expected you to be in bed already. I've got work to do tonight."

"Dad?"

"Yes."

"Dad . . ."

"*What?*"

"You're cranky, never mind."

"Don't do that to me, Isaac. Tell me what you were going to say."

He got into bed and said nothing. I picked out two of the books I had bought him—Don Freeman's *Dandelion* and Patricia Reilly Giff's *Happy Birthday, Ronald Morgan*—and lay down next to him. I looked out of the corner of my eye to see if he looked upset. He didn't look any which way. He had covered his head with his sheet.

I waited for him to reappear.

"C'mon, Isaac, *please*. I've got work to do."

He didn't stir.

"Isaac, I don't have all night." Truly a golden-oldie, *that* one. He came up from under the sheet. "Dad," he protested, "you're not being fair. Act like you usually do when you can't find me."

"I don't want to, Isaac, I'm not in the mood," I told him, approaching in what was left of my mind a new moronic low. I hadn't meant to be such a kill-joy. On the other hand, this barely stifled thought came to mind: You're six years old now, Isaac. Don't you think you should act it? Don't you think you should think of other people's needs? You're not the only person in this world, you know.

Furthermore: You're too old to be playing the silly game where I pretend I don't know where you are and I start looking in strange places, like under the bed, and then I say to Mr. Bear that I'll lie in the middle of the bed and wait for you to get back, and then I accidentally lie on you, and you leap out delightedly and say you fooled me.

"Please, Dad?"

He ducked back under the sheet. I gave in and pretended to look for him. When I gently thrust an elbow into an area under the sheet that I judged to be his ribs, while exclaiming to Mr. Bear that I had looked everywhere for Isaac and didn't know where he was, Isaac emerged giggling and gave me a hug. "You can read to me now, Dad," he suggested gently.

DAD AND SON

I felt better. A happier dad for having played with my kid. But, even while that was so, other phrases, real or imagined, roiled in my memory: "Stop your foolishness," "I don't have time for fooling around," "You're supposed to be a big boy now," "There's no need to cry" (and its more destructive companion, "Big boys don't cry"), "Why are you sniveling?" and "When I was a boy I was already able to . . ." And then there's my mom's inspirational favorite, "You're laughing *now*, but you'll be crying soon." It's my all-time favorite joy smotherer, though honorary mention must be given to its equally motivational near-clone, "You want something to cry about? *I'll* give you something to cry about." My mom, an understanding listener for me when I was little, was also a more memorable phrasemaker than most moms.

The pretend find-me game Isaac and I had just played had taken less than two minutes. It had made Isaac happy. It had made me feel human again. I was grateful that Isaac hadn't given up on the game or on me. They ought to permit euthanasia, I thought, for people who have already put themselves away by believing they're too old to pretend. Besides, Isaac had the rest of his life to become a one-note, monotoned, no-fun adult. If he did become one, of course, I really *would* give him something to cry about.

Men can be silly, I thought. Men *need* to be silly, I corrected myself, and started reading.

Hours later, after having gotten the kids to bed and taken care of my work, I lay on my office bed and remembered with a remorseful heart the really-rotten thing I had said recently to Isaac.

He had been getting a haircut from a woman who comes to our house to cut my hair and his. Isaac used to *hate* getting his hair cut. He said it yanked on his scalp and hurt him. (Ironically, researchers have proved that the scalp *is* more sensitive at age six than at any other age.) It was hard for him to sit still. Or, possibly, he just didn't want to be touched. The biggest problem of all: The back of Isaac's neck was probably the most ticklish spot in the world—except for maybe the front of Isaac's neck.

During this particular haircut, Isaac ducked and gyrated to the point of making haircutting impossible. Teresa told him to sit still or she might accidentally cut his ear. "I don't want this haircut," he said and pulled off the sheet from around his neck.

I was in a writing pit that day, an evil and snarly mood about words and thoughts that refused to join up with one another. "Isaac, I want you to stop this nonsense right away," I said. "You're going to get a haircut, do you understand?" Not real ugly so far. But then I said—it would take me years to forgive myself—"I don't want you walking around looking like a girl."

He threw the sheet back around himself, sat down again and took the rest of his haircut in murderous silence.

I meant to apologize to him immediately after Teresa left. Isaac looked angry, though. Closer to the truth, I was too ashamed to repeat what I had just said.

For the next few months, Isaac complained from time to time that all his curls had been cut off and that he looked ugly.

I never believed that he was talking about his curls or his appearance. I think Isaac felt ugly about himself because of my harsh comment. Little boys spend an inordinate amount of their playtime working out how to look and act and feel like big boys. My comment about Isaac's looking like a girl had been one of the unkindest things I could have said.

I would apologize tomorrow.

I'm sorry, Isaac, I would say. You'll never look like a girl. You'll always look like a dream I had, many years ago, maybe even lifetimes ago, of a boy so special that I would want to grow and live with him forever. I never did speak those words. When I tried to say them about a month later, Isaac cut me off. He said I had never made him feel bad.

FURTHER REFLECTIONS

As the years went by, I never apologized to Isaac. Or, perhaps I did wordlessly, by trying to listen more closely to the ugly feelings about being a little boy still echoing in me. I think that did help. That . . . and having a generously forgiving son who intuitively knows the difference between cruel words said in anger, and cruelty. Isaac gives me a perennial's new flower of hope. Every day. I'm so fortunate that he is my son.

My words to Isaac, "I don't want you looking like a girl," were, and are, horrid. Isaac and I have had many talks since about what it takes for him, a nonathlete, to be accepted by his peers, to feel adequately male. For me, this acceptance takes nothing more than what Isaac is. Male— strikingly different from female in ways I don't understand. Male—notably different in ways of the imagination from other boys. Male—my son. I hope there are enough strata of love accumulated now to keep any cruel words I might speak from seeping down to a place where deep wounds curtail life.

My own dad never said anything cruel to me. More to the point, though, he didn't convey the idea—not early on, it came much later—that I was a good man in his eyes and that I could go forth with that view and blessing into the world.

I wanted words from him—you're a good man, I love you. Or, deeds that meant the same. I wanted this for what seemed forever.

Men kill for this love from their dads. They kill their relationships with other men. They kill their feelings with women. They kill love as their goal, so they won't ever be so abused again, harvesting instead the love-illusions of power or money or sex. They kill their once-natural ability to be loving fathers.

And when men like myself aren't killing, we're lying, however unintentionally. Lying about what we need and want. Lying about women. Lying about our importance and our worth. Lying about what we know, where we've been, what we've accomplished. Lying about who we are.

Most of my life, under the tyrant's heart I've pinned to my chest to put space between me and the women I've tried to love, has lain a grieving heart, one that was not so much broken as missing something vital from a man. A heart without a man, and hence, without a woman.

Under my guise of desired aloneness, my heart talk chattered a near-universal male language: Leave me alone, I don't need you, I don't need anyone. But, then there also was a mourner's internal sigh. Listen. "I want my daddy," it whispers. "Please, try to understand me—I need a daddy before I can love you."

My heart says: "If there isn't a daddy here, you'll get to the places in me where I can't protect myself, and I can't let you do that, for I'm already hurting too bad."

My mom used to say, "Wait till *you* have a son. Then you'll understand."

I understand that if I can simply love Isaac for the male he is, the person he is, I don't need to understand much else.

BANG, MOMMY, YOU'RE DEAD

Isaac was getting ready for bed after a full day of firing his new Ghostbusters gun. It was a Christmas present from my wife's parents. They had paid for it, but I had picked it out. Peace activist that I am, this was still the death-spewing beauty I would have wanted when I was five years old.

My son was crazy about his new weapon. It had the basic configuration of a machine gun, made a loud popping sound when fired, and shot two-inch-high yellow foam bullets which traveled about ten feet unless someone's body parts or possessions interfered with the trajectory.

By the end of the day, all the shooting and killing he had done seemed to have gotten to Isaac. Every time he started to put on a sleeve of his pajama top, his arm straightened and fired. "Pow, pow. Bam, bam, kavoom." Between sleeve tuggings, he shot a Police Academy character. When it wouldn't fall, he picked it up and hurled it against the far wall.

I had killed a lot of evil forces when I was Isaac's age, but there had been too many that refused to fall no matter how many times I shot them. So he definitely had my tacit approval to fire at will. As I left his room to prepare the bottle of juice he still wanted at bedtime, he did just that—blasting away at mighty forces as if the end might be near, all the while expanding his repertoire of death gasps.

By the time I returned, he had gotten himself into his pajamas and under the covers. He looked as innocent as the stuffed companion by his side.

"Mr. Bear [the large, friendly, dentist-jacket-attired bear that he slept with] just had a baby for me," he announced.

I congratulated him.

"There's bad news, too, though," he added.

"Tell me."

"The baby's mother died."

"I'm sorry," I said. "How did she die?"

He ignored my question. "The baby is only one month old. No, only one day old. Could the baby be just one hour old?"

"Sure, we could say the baby was born just an hour ago."

The baby in question was a smallish white polar bear who always wore a red ski cap. Before being born again, he, along with Mr. Bear, had helped Isaac feel safe at night.

After having been knocked off with glee so many times by my mother-loving son, I was curious—not intellectually or sociologically, but strictly in the goofy *National Enquirer* sense of the word—about how Isaac had brought about the mother bear's demise. I persisted in my questioning in the scarcely concealed guise of a homicide groupie.

"How did the bear's mother die?" I tried again.

"She was smoking a cigarette during lunch, blew the smoke onto her bologna sandwich, ate the sandwich and choked to death. The bologna and smoke got stuck halfway down her throat. That was it for her."

"Tough way to go. I'm sorry." I wasn't. I was delighted to be the sole surviving parent for once.

In three days, I was going to take Isaac on our first day-trip in my new stand-and-drive step van. It would be Isaac's first time traveling with me when his mom wasn't driving us. I was very moved to be accompanied by a tiny bear born of a man bear, with no mom around to take care of him. At the same time, the memory of my trying futilely for a full two years to be able to walk Zoe a mere twenty yards from our backyard to a crabapple tree near the front of our house crippled my confidence. A month ago, I had been unable to sit long enough to make it through a meal at a restaurant. I had stood at tables the few times we ate dinner at restaurants, loathing the gawking and staring, and the embarrassment I felt my children suffered. I had my truck now, but I was still learning to master driving it and, even more, getting my body working well enough to take longer trips.

This fretting faded with the sunshine of being with Isaac, Mr. Bear and Baby Bear. I delighted in the two-hour drive to visit friends of mine. Getting there was manageable. Being there was a joy. Isaac seemed bolder than usual. Until today, he always had panicked about any dog that tried to jump up on him. Now, when my friends' Shetland sheepdog leaped onto his chest, Isaac laughed, grabbed the dog's front paws and started to dance with him. Then, after a few minutes of staying near me, he wandered off for a couple of hours with my friends' two older kids. Later, when I stepped out the back door to tell him we were leaving, I watched him coming headfirst down a slide, something he had been afraid to try at home.

On our way home, when I pulled off the road to rest and uncramp my muscles, Isaac talked at length about building a home of his own right inside a big apartment building near where my friends lived. He also would buy a step van and come out to visit me on weekends. He would move his room, or maybe our entire house, on a flatbed truck and have it put inside his apartment building. He even would make a backyard and pool for his apartment building if I thought the people who owned the town wouldn't mind.

When we got home, Zoe was upset about not having gone with us. (This first trip with me had been hers to make, as the older child, but she had declined, concerned, she said, that she would miss her mom too much.) She badgered Isaac until, ten minutes after our arrival, he broke down. He sat on the bottom step of our staircase, tears streaming. "I'll never be able to be a father," he protested. "The whole thing is impossible. I'll never be able to grow up if certain people are going to be mad at me for not being a baby."

When calm was finally restored, we all wound up on Zoe's bed to discuss the day. Zoe apologized to Isaac and said she wanted to go someplace the following weekend with me; she and I made a plan to spend a day away.

As we continued our discussion on Zoe's bed, I noticed that Isaac had gotten quiet. He seemed to be working hard at orchestrating his fingers, trying out a new trick he had learned, a trick that every boy learns or maybe knows from birth, where you make a trigger out of your thumb and middle finger and use your index finger as a gun barrel.

"Could I shoot someone with real bullets like this?" he spoke quietly, looking at me.

"You mean could bullets come out of your finger?"

"Yes."

"No, it couldn't happen."

"Even if I wished hard?"

"It's unlikely," I said.

More to the point, I saw that while he was asking me about the possibility of real bullets coming out of his finger, he had aimed the finger in question at his mom. I waited to see if he would pull the trigger.

He did.

She didn't notice.

"Bang, you're dead," he mumbled softly. He watched her closely for a few seconds. She kept talking. He smiled.

A little later, at bedtime, Isaac lay in his mom's arms and wept, speech thick with life in conflict, mourning the day he would have to leave her and live so far away when he moved near my friends' house.

The next evening, when we found ourselves standing around in Isaac's room at bedtime, he declared that his fireman's hat was a crystal ball. Staring at it with psychic aplomb, he had us sit down while he gave forth his prognostications:

"Mommy, you'll live one more year, then you'll be eaten by a lion."

"Zoe, you'll live five centuries."

"Dad, do you want to know your future?"

"Sure," I said, resisting the urge to ask for a cigarette and a last meal.

He peered deeply into his crystal ball, this son of mine, past and future master of the dramatic pause. "You'll live a million years and always be our father," he intoned.

FURTHER REFLECTIONS

Isaac is closer to his mom now than he was at age five.

Perhaps one reason for this is that Dava and I separated a year ago, and our living apart has made it easier for Isaac to know Dava at her best. I don't know whether his childhood notion of shooting her with bullets hurtling from his fingertips has a preadolescent parallel. I do know he gets murderously angry with me. But that's another story, the next chapter.

No doubt, little kids hate parents, certain foods and early bedtimes at one point or another. I don't remember, though, being angry at my mother when I was a kid. I just recall hoping that she would be around and not be so sad.

My older sister was something of a mom to me, though, and I did try to do her in when I was four. Flung myself across the room at her after a provocation I don't remember, and bit her in the stomach, leaving her with a bad laceration and a bunch of tooth marks. My sister screamed. My mother got hysterical. After I realized I would live in spite of my attempted murder, I felt surprisingly unrepentant, even pleased, about what I had done. Actually, I felt *really* good.

If I never did get mad at my mom—and no one in my family has any memory to the contrary—I seem to have found myself a substitute mom to rage at in my first marriage. My first wife went into an emotional tailspin shortly after we married, reminiscent of my mom's depression after I was born. I grew increasingly angry at her. I felt it was my responsibility to keep her world intact. To be her world.

My anger felt larger than I was as the months of married life went by. I reminded myself that my father had successfully doused his reputedly terrible temper; I wanted to kill off mine.

About two years into this marriage, at age twenty-eight, my anger, last seen gnawing at my sister, arose from its seemingly unyielding moorings with a terrifying combustive energy I didn't think I could control.

I was in the kitchen of our twentieth-floor apartment on the upper west side of Manhattan. I had taken an apple out of the fruit bin and was having trouble getting the bin to slide back into the refrigerator. I cursed and shoved to no avail. Kicked at it. Then asked my wife to help. She knew of my ineptitude with things mechanical. It was a sensitive issue. She yelled from the living room, "If you can't be the man in this family, who is supposed to be?"

I felt like someone else. I pictured a detonated grenade spitting lethal wire fragments. I walked fast toward my wife in the living room. She got up quickly out of her chair. Although we were the same height, I managed to clasp her shoulders very tightly and lift her a few inches off the ground. I started to walk her backwards slowly, her feet kicking, toward the bay window that peered out left and right at the Central Park Reservoir and Hudson River.

I vaguely heard her screaming to put her down. Only my inner screaming could be heard clearly. At the window, I turned right toward the bedroom, realizing I had been thinking about killing my wife, and somehow had, with what seemed like reason and deliberation, decided not to.

Her screaming reached me now and I dropped her. She fell to the floor and accused me of trying to kill her.

When I think back now about Isaac's pretending to shoot his mom, it feels better than ever to me. It takes too much anger to contain anger.

Too much anger contains love, too.

DROP DEAD, DAD

It wouldn't have mattered whether I had just read the latest popular articles on the subject or even devoted my career to being a child psychoanalyst.

I still would have been a bit shocked to discover that the little fellow I had cuddled, burped, bathed, protected from monsters and held to my heart blatantly wanted Mommy.

Not *wanted Mommy* as in "Isaac wanted Mommy to sing him a lullaby."

I mean *really* wanted Mommy.

Romantically wanted Mommy.

Until I took this in, I had figured Freud for a seminal thinker. But only about other people's kids.

A healthy, well-adjusted kid, *my* kid, wasn't going to want to bed down with his mother. That was textbook theory. Isaac and I were close. We could talk. This phase of growing up shouldn't be a big deal. For example, if Isaac had unseemly thoughts about Dava, he might say to me, "Hey, Dad, Mommy is pretty." I would say, "She sure is, Isaac, and when you get older, you'll find a girl just like Mommy to marry." He would consider that fact, be somewhat in awe of my judgment and conclude, "Golly, Dad, you're right; besides, Mommy is *your* wife." "Attaboy, you got the picture now," I would encourage. It would be nothing short of a simpatico synchrony of loving feelings.

This Oedipus business wasn't going to happen. Isaac and I *under-stood* each other. I had always spent time with him. I was more comfortable with intimacy than were my chary male progenitors. It was even fine with me that Isaac was already better than I in some ways—for example, at understanding anything spatial and at being engagingly outgoing and outrageously charming. I was no Competitive Macho Dad. Isaac was no Crazed Oepidal Son. We were cool.

That's what I believed when Isaac was three. When he was three and a half, I thought: *Oedipus lives.*

Neither my wife nor I was ready for Isaac's first headfirst leap into mommy-wanting. We were expecting a tentative step in that direction at most. We were wrong. I was lying on Isaac's bed, about to read him a story the first time he let fly. Dava walked into the room.

"Would you like to sleep with me all night?" Isaac asked her.

"What do you mean?" she asked, seemingly stunned.

"You know, sleep with me all night," Isaac repeated.

"Well, sure," Dava said. She *was* stunned. Stunned, zapped, gone goodbye.

I realized I had been biting on Isaac's bedtime book while listening to their conversation. "What your mom means," I butted in, "is that she wants to sleep with *me* and have you comfortable sleeping in *your* room *by yourself*." Dava, composed once more, concurred with this reality.

The next evening, when I went upstairs, I came upon Isaac helping Dava make our bed. The scene reminded me that he had spent most of the day "playing house" with Zoe and carrying around and caring for a doll named Annie. I had never seen him pay this much attention to a doll before. Zoe had been caring for her My Child doll; Isaac had been the helpful hubby.

When Isaac saw me, he asked Dava, "This is my and your bed, isn't it, Mommy?" I gave him an arched-eyebrow look. He recanted, "No, this is *your* bed, Daddy, yours and Mommy's, isn't it?" I agreed it was.

Normal stuff, right? No big deal. Certainly no grown man could get angry at his son for indulging in some routine fantasy about Mommy.

So I thought.

The next day, a glorious summer Saturday morning that lent itself to smiles all around, Isaac asked me to show him how to use a *harriet*. A hatchet, he meant.

I pondered the potential symbolism, not to mention the risk to my life, and decided that a hatchet was sometimes just a hatchet, especially if it was a seriously dulled hatchet like the one I had buried somewhere in the garage.

I found the hatchet. And Zoe, Isaac and I went out to do some hatcheting. After a few whacks directed by me at a fairly slender branch I had selected for its fragile appearance, I realized I should have put a board under it. The ground was soft from rain, and the branch was sinking into it and making artistic impressions, but not splitting. I also realized that my body wasn't going to function much longer at this activity. My right elbow, which years of muscle cramping had torn away at, was ablaze. I kept hacking away, though, until the kids' insistent chorus of requests to take a turn made me a trifle impatient.

I ranted gently, "Just wait a minute, damn it. Let me show you how to split wood. Maybe you'll learn something."

That quieted them down. It also made me feel like an s.o.b., so I decided to give them a turn. It was lesson time from the master. I flipped a coin in order to stifle the chorus of "I go first, no I do, you went first last year, yeah but you . . ." Isaac got the honor.

After a terse, grouchy lecture from me on hatchet safety—basically, one should never cut off one's vital body parts without a note from one's parents, and furthermore, one should be *very* careful—I held the hatchet with Isaac and we jointly began to chip away at the now-all-but-earth-covered branch.

After a while, I backed off and let Isaac try swinging the hatchet by himself. He was surprisingly tentative. It seemed to me that he was taking my lecture *too* seriously, so I suggested he try a more vigorous upswing. When he continued to tap lightly at the branch, I again held the hatchet with him and tried to demonstrate what I meant. Which is how I accidentally helped him hit himself in the forehead with the blunt end of the hatchet.

Instantly, a lump began to form. I apologized with a grieving heart. Isaac cried briefly, shunned my apology, stormed into the house and wound up in his mom's lap. Coincidence or not, before the day was over, he had suffered two more mishaps. Once when he got up from under the bathroom sink and cracked his head on the edge of it. The second time when we took him to look at a fancy, wooden swing set; somehow the swing-chair came flying after Isaac after he disembarked, hitting him in the temple and all but knocking him cold.

DAD AND SON

The intellect has nothing worthwhile to say at moments like these. It tells you, for example, that you're not to blame for the three black-and-blue swellings symmetrically situated on your son's head. But you pay no attention to your intellect, especially when your gut tells you that bad things happen to good sons when they have stupid dads.

That night, during the time reserved for our snuggle after a bedtime story, Isaac gyrated his body away from me as far as he could, raised his legs onto the wall and rested his feet there. I felt he would have pushed the wall down and rolled fetally away from me into a new life if he could have. On the other hand, perhaps not certain he wanted to be this alone, Isaac groped around with one hand behind him until he found my neck. He nestled his hand there. I put my hand over his, gave it a gentle squeeze, got up and said my goodnights. He didn't respond. Not a word. It was the first time he had said nothing to me at bedtime since he had first learned to talk. It was also the first time since he was an infant that he had no kiss for me.

A week later, Dava left on a business trip to England, and that afternoon, I took the kids to the beach. We had a good time playing running bases and collecting rocks and shells. I was getting back to my feet after having gathered up our paraphernalia when something hard crashed into my face. The force knocked me off balance into the sand. I was badly frightened because the eye that had been operated on a few weeks before, for cataracts caused by my neuromuscular condition, had absorbed some of the blow.

I looked around. The hurled object in question was a fairly hard orange ball. The hurler, from point-blank range, was Isaac. "How could you *do* that to me?" I screamed at him. He looked unconcerned, devoid of trembling lip or tears, his face a mask I never had seen before. He continued to stare at me, which further infuriated me. I looked again and realized the mask he wore had a name. It was hatred, the Grade A extra-pure variety. I had never seen it before on his face.

My injured eye was weeping uncontrollably. Trying to regain my composure, I focused on wondering what might be behind Isaac's hostile action. I imagined myself as Isaac. You're much bigger than I, I might say. You have Mommy. You can do tricks with a ball. You show off and make me feel small and horrible. So stick it in your eye. Maybe that was it. But I was too furious to care. Parents are just as talented as kids at hating loved ones, and at that moment, I wanted to murder Isaac. Instead, I grounded him—no television or electronic games for a week.

I fumed and despaired the rest of the day. Isaac moped. Zoe worried about my eye, which was a bit worse for wear, but not seriously damaged.

That evening at bedtime, in the middle of my reading, Isaac whispered something to me. I thought I heard him but I couldn't believe the words. I asked him to repeat them. "I'd like to hit you in the head with a hammer," he said.

I sat up. "Are you out of your mind?" I asked.

"No," Isaac replied. "I meant hit you *gently* in the head, Dad."

"Uh huh," I said. "Well, forget about it, Isaac, because I'm not going to let you do anything like that. I've got to be in one piece this week, not all mashed in, to take care of you and Zoe. And I will be, got it? And if I hear one more word like that from you, there will be hell to pay. Got that, too?"

He seemed to get it. He gave me a goodnight kiss.

I went into Zoe's room. She immediately cheered me up by offering to get a cold compress for my eye. I thanked her, assured her I was fine and started reading to her. Isaac came into the room.

"What's up?" I asked him.

"I had to pee again. Would you tuck me back in?"

I apologized to Zoe for the interruption and went with Isaac.

"Dad, what were you doing in my room a few minutes ago?" he asked as I was straightening his tangled sheet and blanket. Before I had started reading to Zoe, I had made a quick trip to Isaac's room to turn on the portable intercom that linked up to my office. He had seemed to be asleep at the time.

I told him about the intercom. "You're absent minded. You already had turned it on," he said.

"No, I hadn't, Isaac." I finished tucking him in. "You've been really crummy today, you know."

"What does crummy mean?" he asked.

"You've acted badly . . . at times horribly," I said.

"Am I acting badly with you?"

"Yes, that's the point. What's with you? Are you upset that Mommy is away?"

"Why should I be? She's been away before."

"I'm aware of that, Isaac. But she's never been away for six nights." I added, "Just in case you're wondering, I didn't send her away. She had to go on a business trip."

"She *had* to go?"

"Yes, we both have to make trips at times. If we don't travel, we don't make money."

"Oh," he said. "Thanks, Dad."

Two days later, two days of Isaac being my loving son again, I went up to his room and handed him his bedtime drink. "The right parent didn't do the right thing," he said.

I was almost too tired to care what that meant, but being a curiosity glutton, I asked. "What does that mean?"

"It means the right thing to do with Mommy away would have been to turn yourself into a mommy."

Nice. Besides, who had time these days for sex-change surgery? The little so-and-so, who had just told me he was sleeping in his birthday suit to be like me, was at it again. He wasn't embarrassed about it, either. He looked me right in the eye. "Now the *really* right thing," he went on enthusiastically, "would be for Zoe and me to have two mommies and no daddy."

Rotten kid.

He turned his back to the wall while I read. Then cheerily climbed on my back while I put on my shoes. I piggybacked him to the bathroom and walked into Dava's and my bedroom to wait for him.

"Dad," he yelled within seconds from the bathroom. "Could you give me a piggyback ride back to bed?"

"You can walk, Isaac," I said.

"Please, Dad?"

I managed to keep the obscenities that unexpectedly found their way out of my mouth fairly low in volume and walked into the bathroom. "Okay, climb on," I said.

He did, wrapping his arms around me real tight and giving me a big, wet kiss on the back of my neck. "I love you, Dad," he said.

Rotten kid.

Rotten kid who happened to give good kisses.

DROP DEAD, DAD

FURTHER REFLECTIONS

When I wrote "Drop Dead, Dad," what I saw mostly as a story about my son's Oedipal phase now feels more like a chronicle of unacknowledged anger.

I forgot how much happened that wasn't funny. My memory diverted the ball thrown into my face. Forgot Isaac's expressed wish to cave in my head with a hammer. Buried Isaac's wanting two moms and no dad. Denied, in general, the anger that stakes out permanently deeded territory in me, and can grow and crisscross other internal areas and boundaries with ease at times.

At three and a half, Isaac's anger was difficult for me to take. Illness had displaced my skin with little more than a held breath; Isaac's anger went directly to my heart. I was hurt, enraged at times, that he seemed to hate me. I wish I hadn't been so easily offended. I still struggle with, as Zoe has pointed out, "taking things too personally."

Isaac's anger was direct then. A ball thrown. Feet kicking me away while I read. A kiss withheld.

Direct is better. Easier to live with than anger flipsided into depression and pain, Isaac's or mine. This other kind of anger started up a year ago, when I moved out of the home Isaac had grown up in. I hadn't wanted to leave, but Dava and I couldn't agree on another way. Isaac knew I didn't want to leave him. But knowing often has no relevance except for test-taking. Head loses to heart. I *had* left him.

On the plus side for me, the family warring started losing its hold on me the moment I left. The same was true for Zoe. Not so for Isaac, who waged war for a resumption of war.

Parents spank kids and leave marriages and tell kids it's for their good. Isaac wasn't buying it. I wasn't there for him as much. I couldn't mediate turbulence every day as I once had. I couldn't apply as many emotional bandages. I felt Isaac's hatred of me for these lacks in his life.

Genetic inevitability had stopped with me, I thought. Isaac and I had talked from the first. And now we weren't. He looked at his feet or past my eyes. Mumbled curses. Mimicked my speech. Spent hours without talking—a mime of rage. It took almost nine months. Then: talking and more talking. A lap snuck into once in a while. Sitting on a couch, guiding my arm around his shoulders. More talking. The old love growing into something new and different—never to be the same again.

I'm left with hope. And two crazy thoughts about anger. First, that expressing it should be everyone's inalienable right, and more, obligation. No choice—out with it. I was afraid to do that when I was a kid. Isaac did it at age three and put it on a shelf that couldn't hold it at ten.

Second, there's abusiveness in a child's unexpressed anger. Parental abusiveness. Parents taking away the option of anger from a child is cruel —and as easy as counting to three—a word, a shrug, a gesture. It's the ultimate cruelty, because it forbids healing and denies humanness. It leaves wreckage—worse, a void—where love might dwell.

There are two rules in my men's group: Bring yourself, as much of your self as possible to meetings. And, no violence. The men bring every-thing, certainly anger. Not abstract anger. Not mourning anger. But freshly made anger at each other. The wonder of it. Every time it happens, we grow as a group.

About Isaac's anger: It's still hard to take, but I think it's one of the best gifts I've given him and me.

RAISING MYSELF

TOUCHING

It was Isaac's bedtime. He had turned three the week before. I lay on the bed next to him, my hand absent-mindedly caressing the back of his curly head.

He mumbled sleepily, "Put your hand lower."

I wasn't sure what he meant so I moved my hand to his shoulder.

"That's not it," he said, in a voice so gruff it startled me.

I didn't know what to do.

"Daddy, you don't understand," he said. He took my hand, removed it from his shoulder and pressed it gently to his cheek. The moment my hand touched there he fell asleep.

I didn't want to risk waking him. And, moments later, after he was sleeping soundly, the feeling of caressing his cheek with my hand was so sweet I didn't want to leave.

I lay there without moving. I felt warm and afloat with love. Tears gathered and it was all I could do to not cry aloud.

If you were awake, I told Isaac silently, you would be asking me one of your wonderful *why* questions. Why are you crying, Dad? After I explained, you would say, yes but why does being happy make a person cry?

My words wouldn't tell you much, but you would look at my face and I think you would understand.

Better that you're asleep. I talk a good game of it being fine for boys and men to cry, but I would be flustered if you opened your eyes at this moment. God forbid you should think me weak.

My hand still caressing Isaac's cheek, I drifted back to when he was fifteen months old. We took our first walk together then. It was on our front lawn. Isaac had been walking for barely a month and I hadn't been out of bed walking for much longer than that. He was all wobbly excited, more movement than forward motion, grasping one of my hands with his.

We made our way together to a big tree on the lawn. He paused there. Then he took my hand he was holding and pressed it to his cheek and held it there. I thought at that instant I would never feel unloved again.

This hand of Isaac's, this boy's hand, so primordially and reflexively fond of hurling stones, brandishing swords, forming temporary homes for bugs, grabbing, examining, hitting, spilling, building, curling into different weapon shapes . . .

This boy's hand could love.

I never spoke to Isaac during these hand-to-cheek moments.

There is a sense of eternal comfort, but you can't express it, when your heart is in another's hand.

Isaac thrives on physical contact. I never knew how to ask for that myself. The notion collided with one of my family's myths, "Artie doesn't like to be touched." I didn't. I'm not sure I understand why.

I remember, at age four in my parents' bedroom, trying to flee my mother's touch when she wanted to pinch my tush.

When I was ten, dressed for Sunday school, my dad wanted to adjust my tie and collar and I wriggled away from him. I apparently had done this several times in the past because he said, "How am I supposed to help you if you won't ever let anyone touch you?"

In my early twenties, at a Passover Seder at my parents' house, a man my dad's age got up during the meal, walked over to his son's chair and kissed him on the cheek. I had never seen that happen—a dad kissing his adult son. I found it odd; I thought the two men peculiar. The son looked pleased. He is a state supreme court judge today, and as unfounded and even downright foolish as this may sound, I'm certain he is a more loving and compassionate judge because of his father's affection.

When I was forty-seven, my parents were leaving my family's home after a visit. I was holding Isaac in my arms and kissing him. My father, smiling, watched us with wet eyes. I put Isaac down and embraced my father. He held me close in return. It was the first time since I was a little boy that he had allowed me to hug him.

When Isaac was a baby, I developed the habit of placing my hand on his chest after reading to him, just at the moment he was ready for sleep. I would rest my right palm on his pajama-covered chest and spread my fingers wide. My fingers would span nearly his entire chest wall, from his heart to the lowest portion of his rib cage. In my hand, every night, I could feel the heartbeat, the endurance as well as the temporalness of my son's life. I also could feel the need for touch in my infant son. My need, too. It was one of countless ways I was learning to be a father—to Isaac as well as to myself.

At age three, Isaac began to get out of his chair during dinner, sometimes right after dinner, too, and sit in my lap. I would wrap my arms around him—"not too tight, Dad" he often would say—and squeeze and inhale him as one might a loaf of homebaked bread. When he would climb off, it was with a casualness that bespoke, "It's not that I needed your old lap, Dad; I just thought your knees were cold and lonely."

A different kind of touching started when Isaac was four. That's when he first began wanting to wrestle with me after dinner. Zoe often joined us. I took turns with them, playing with them on the living room rug, teaching them the few moves I remembered from intramural wrestling at Lehigh University, where I once had dreamed of catching up enough with the school's innumerable state champions to make the junior varsity team at 123 pounds. I never made it. But this roughhousing with my kids was glory enough and then some.

Wrestling with my kids was more than affectionate messing around for us. It also was reassurance—as much for me as for them—that Dad was strong enough to throw them around yet keep them safe.

Once, Isaac and I even wrestled for a small audience. It was one of the last times he permitted me, no less encouraged me, to maul him lovingly in public view.

He was in kindergarten. I drove over to pick him up at school and waited for him near the front door. When he bounded out and spotted me, he took off his book bag, gave me a big grin and started making wrestling takedown motions.

DAD AND SON

I crouched and waved him on. He took a few running steps and landed in my arms, where he snuggled for a moment. Then, with a loud whoop, he yanked off my hat, threw it on the ground, wriggled free, slid down one leg and clasped his arms around it.

I eased us both down to the ground and the match was on. The kindergartners who were waiting for their parents to pick them up formed a circle around us, yelling words of encouragement to Isaac. When he pinned me after a prolonged struggle, they cheered.

About this time, Isaac worked out a new routine at bedtime. He was inspired producer, director and luminary. "Dad, you kneel here beside my bed and I'll climb onto your shoulders. Carry me like this into yours and Mom's bedroom. Sit on that bed. When you do, I'll fling myself backwards off your shoulders and bounce on the mattress. Now, here comes the really good part. Back away a few steps from the bed—are you *sure* this is safe, Dad?—and I'll leap into your arms. Then you whirl me around a few times and throw me back onto the bed again. How's that sound?"

Sounds good, I said. I extended the routine after the final fling by carrying Isaac piggyback into the bathroom, where I left him for a final bedtime pee, learning the hard way (hard for Isaac) that before I slid him off my back onto the closed toilet seat, I had to remember to get my hairbrush out of my back pocket. He reminded me often and somewhat irritably about this after a minor mishap.

Six months before my friend Carl, Isaac's godfather, died of AIDS in March 1991, I went to visit him in the hospital.

It was the worst I had seen him. One of his arms was massively infected. His diarrhea was uncontrolled. His body and mind were so pained he could barely talk except to say he wanted to sleep.

Carl Thiele and I had been friends for twenty-two years. In 1970, he was the national advertising director of *Library Journal* and I the promotion director at the *New York Times* school and library division. We met about business and immediately became friends. I knew Carl, and his wife and children, for five years before he told me he was gay. Our friendship continued to grow. He was an uncommonly decent, intelligent and warm man. I loved him dearly.

I pulled my chair as close to Carl's bed as it would go and stroked his hair. His smile was beautiful, but his color was ebbing toward death. He

TOUCHING

held out his hand for me to hold. I held it, scarcely moving, for two hours while he slept.

Six months later, on the day before Carl died, I took his hand one last time. He brought my hand to his cheek, held it there and closed his eyes. He never opened them again. I was crying too hard to see his face. But his touch remains with me to this day.

KILLING CHIPMUNKS, NURSING HAMSTERS

I still enjoy popping soda and beer cans off perches with BB and pellet guns. But I don't hunt anymore and probably would no longer kill anything unless I had to.*

Ever since Isaac turned four and expressed horror that so many people who believe in God needlessly kill life that He created, I've even stopped swatting bugs in the bedroom and spraying ants in the kitchen. At least when Isaac is around.

Years ago, though, there were two periods of my life when nothing was more satisfying than hunting. Once when I was a preteen. The other time when I was much younger than that emotionally, trying to feel like a man again after years of being incapacitated.

When I was ten, my friend Rocky Stone showed me how to make a slingshot out of wire hangers and thick elastic bands. About twice a week for the next two years, Rocky and I hunted in the swamp and woods behind my house. We shot at anything small that hopped, flew, climbed or slithered. Our arsenal, which we concealed from my parents in our grungy, violence-feeding pockets, consisted of small rocks, marbles that we didn't want anymore and BBs that we stole from the local sporting goods store.

---

*I want to note, however, that the outdoorsmen I know who have grown up with hunting often show greater respect for life than do men who protest all hunting activities.

KILLING CHIPMUNKS, NURSING HAMSTERS

For the first year, we missed everything living we shot at. It didn't matter, though. It was the hunt and the camaraderie we loved. We were warriors! Girls could (and did) laugh at us. *Silly boys pretending to be hunters.* Men guffawed. *Unusual slingshots you have there, boys.* But squirrels showed us chattering respect. They screeched like indignant yentas when we entered their territory with our cocked wire hangers at the ready. Seeing them leap from branch to branch as our missiles landed even remotely near them pumped us up. Today's video games may involve kids in mindless violence, but the games are neither as mindless nor as violent as Rocky's and my pursuit of obligingly dare-devil squirrels.

They were our favorite target. But we also shot at everything from snakes to birds to our own jumping feet. Then one day, out of probably thousands of shots I had taken at birds, one BB landed with an alarmingly loud thunk in the belly of a sparrow flying directly over my head. She was no more than twenty feet up. I can still picture the scene in detail—where I stood next to marsh weeds on ground mucky with our footprints, the bird's white stomach, my shrieking "I got it," the red blotch on the bird's stomach, elation, agitation, dread. Rocky's silence and the undetermin-able look behind his foggy glasses.

I felt sweaty and lightheaded. The bird didn't plunge to the ground. It cried out, flew crazily in small circles, then half-glided, half-fell into a clump of bushes near us. My immediate thought was to bring it home. Not tell my parents what had happened. Nurse it back to health as I had tried to do a few months before with a baby rabbit my dog had brought me. I had kept the rabbit alive in spite of its badly damaged neck by feeding it warm milk from a baby's bottle and mashed wild raspberries by hand. On the third morning, though, when I went out to the garage to take care of it, it was dead, lying stiffly on its side on a soft blanket near the light bulb meant to keep it warm. I didn't want the bird to die, too. I kept searching for it, almost stepping on its head when I finally came upon it. Its eyes were open but it wasn't moving. It had been killed by a single BB, the fall, the scare. I had killed it.

Several years later, I went trapshooting on weekends with Rocky. A few years after that I fired an M-1 rifle as an Army reservist. But I never did any more hunting until I invented a bizarre, new version of the sport when Zoe was two and a half years old.

DAD AND SON

I was just getting back on my feet at the time, barely able to be out of bed for half an hour at a time. And what I wanted more than anything else—ever—was to be a dad, not an invalid, in Zoe's eyes.

I didn't understand, yet, that an invalid *can* retain a sense of self and that *I* hadn't. Or that a young child with a disabled father *can* love him and that Zoe did. Things had gone badly in our family during my illness; our feelings about it never were discussed. I felt isolated from Zoe. So much so that I went for a childlike grandstand play. Look at Daddy, Zoe. He's tough because he can shoot and kill.

One summer evening, I found my old Daisy pump gun and showed it to Zoe. It was as harmless a weapon as ever was—old, difficult to pump, barely able to penetrate a thin sheet of cardboard pumped to its maximum, but a symbol I found myself clinging to.

I talked to Zoe about guns and about having served in the Army, exaggerating these landmarks of my manhood. I told her about the 30-30 rifle I had bought a year before, explaining that it shot real bullets and that I could kill someone with it *now*.

Zoe was fascinated. Could Daddy shoot a bad man if he tried to harm Zoe? Yes. Daddy may not be able to run or do much else, but he can protect Zoe, I told her.

The next evening after dinner, I started using my BB pistol to take target practice at beer cans. Every evening thereafter that summer, when the weather was nice, Zoe would eagerly anticipate my shooting exhibition. The look on her face when I knocked down a can was little-girl admiring. Until now, her fear of my illness had guarded that look. I was delighted.

I can't remember exactly how it started, but after a few weeks, my after-dinner target practice took on aspects of a hunt, complete with retrieving dog.

There were dozens of chipmunks in our backyard. Some of them were probably the same ones I had fed by hand when they were babies. I had moved to this house after my first marriage ended. Before breakfast each morning, I would go out back and encourage clusters of chickadees to land on my shoulders and palms to get sunflower seeds. After breakfast, families of chipmunks would come to the back door for me to fingerfeed them cheese, raisins and birdseed.

After I became ill, a builder told me that my beloved chipmunks were menaces; living close to the house they would eat through the outside-wall shingles. It hadn't happened but no matter. The rumor helped me justify taking potshots at the chipmunks whenever they scurried near my beer-can targets.

My aim got uncannily accurate, especially for someone who had barely made marksman in the Army, starting as a Private and departing as same. Enter Rover (officially: Rover Rah Rah, so named by Zoe—the "rah rah" her imitation of a barking sound). Rover was fluffy and floppy and wildly friendly, a cacophonous Benjy who loved to chase cars and hunt chipmunks.

Rover and I became hunters in tandem. Whenever a chipmunk ran across the wooden fence outside our back door, I would knock it down with a well-placed BB and Rover would bark like a madman and chase it across the yard until it was treed. Stretching his front paws as far up the trunk as he could, he would unleash a furious clamor, as if his full repertoire of sounds alone—throaty growls, yips and bazooka barks— could untree the chipmunk. Anywhere from twenty to thirty feet up, panting in terror on a branch, would be our prey.

I now would try to dislodge the chipmunk from the tree with a shot to the rump. When I succeeded, Rover would chase the chipmunk and sometimes kill it by stomping it with one of his clublike paws.

Five years after I took my last potshot at a small animal, one of the two hamsters that my wife and I had gotten Zoe for her eighth birthday, Harry the Hamster, developed medical problems.

Harry was kind and cuddly, plump and magnificently reddish brown. Cloned and curled in a sleeping position, he would be one of the few pairs of earmuffs you could wear with pride. Harry was exceptionally gentle. He never bit anyone or even attacked his cage companion, Larry. By contrast, Larry bit Harry occasionally, and, on the second day we owned him, punctured the fingertip of one of Zoe's friends so deeply that it took me an hour to staunch the bleeding.

I was especially fond of Harry. He was two years old, senior citizen status for a hamster, when I noticed that the hingelike apparatus on the right side of his jaw seemed to have been bitten, and broken, by Larry during the night. When Harry stood up on his hind legs against a side of his cage, waiting for a lettuce snack, he could only close his jaw over the food with great effort. A few days later he began to lose fur on his face and legs.

I made some calls, found the one vet within fifty miles who treated hamsters and took Harry to see him.

Dr. Claude Grosjean, as handsomely French as his name, told me that he had bred hamsters as a child. He diagnosed Harry as having a broken and possibly infected jaw and gave me a bottle of antibiotic medication.

Zoe and I made a plan to try to save Harry's life, complete with twice-a-day dosings of the antibiotic and lots of attention, especially holding and petting Harry and letting him nestle and run around on Zoe's chest and stomach.

In spite of our efforts, Harry's condition grew worse. He was still active, but his loss of fur had now progressed to almost half his body. I returned to Dr. Grosjean with Harry and my theory of vitamin deficiency, opining that Harry might be losing fur because of nutrients missing in the instant, easy-to-chew banana-flavored oatmeal we were feeding him in order to not aggravate his broken jaw. Dr. Grosjean bought my theory and prescribed a vitamin supplement.

Every night, Zoe and I prepared treats for Harry and spent even more time with him. We now fed him unflavored oatmeal in case the artificial banana flavoring had been the problem. Just to feel I was doing something extra, I also applied aloe vera to the mangelike sores that were developing on Harry's legs and back and brushed brewer's yeast into his remaining fur.

Harry now looked more like a scabrous, sickly mouse than a hamster. His body was rough to the touch, his movements slow. It became emotionally difficult, then impossible, for Zoe to pick him up. She hung in with me, though, visiting and caring for Harry daily.

We began talking about Harry's impending death. And how neither we nor Dr. Grosjean knew what was wrong with him. And how, although most people want in the worst way to believe that "someone must have an answer," it often isn't the case.

Zoe and I also began talking of the years I had been ill and how frightening for her my sickly appearance must have been. When I told her I thought that a good deal of the fear and anger she had felt toward me back then might be going away, she nodded in agreement. We both cried a bit about how especially unfortunate it was that we hadn't been able to really hug and talk to each other until Zoe was five years old.

One day when we were spending time with Harry, Zoe broke down. She cried for a long time. I suggested we go out in the backyard and choose a site where we could start a family-pet graveyard and bury Harry when the time came. Zoe chose the area, a lovely, sunny plot near our vegetable garden, with a boundary fence and meadow behind it. She situated a gravestone, a triangular shard of a large limestone brick, to mark where we would bury Harry.

We stood there staring at the grave site. I felt depleted. My near-death a few years before seemed to reinhabit me. I silently pleaded against imminent harm or death for all pets and other living creatures near and dear to Zoe.

I needed a break from this whole ghastly subject of medical ailments. But there weren't many respites. My close friend, Isaac's godfather, was dying of AIDS. My mother was in pain most of the time and needing support and advice. My wife's mother had lung-cancer surgery coming up. The cop who drove me to business meetings had died suddenly in his mid-forties. Our family dentist, a man I admired greatly, had just passed away.

More to the point, the only point, Zoe had been forced to confront dying and death far too much. I felt that the first five years of her life had pivoted tormentedly around questions no child should have to continually face: "Will Daddy die? If not, why doesn't he get up? Why doesn't he let *me* be the small, frightened one? Why doesn't he become the dad I need?"

The next morning, I dressed quickly and went to see how Harry was doing. He hadn't eaten much. Worse, he wasn't responding to my presence. I had a lot of work to do that day. No time, really, for a near-dead hamster. Just let the inevitable happen, I told myself. I can't do that to Zoe, I argued back. Harry is Zoe's pet. Harry is love, suffering, living. Harry is an icebreaker. During the past two years, probably a hundred friends, relatives and baby-sitters had visited him and Larry in response to Zoe's greeting at the front door—"Hi, would you like to come up and see my hamsters?" You don't walk away from that much feeling without losing part of yourself.

I called the vet, got a sympathetic response and put Harry into a Buster Brown shoebox filled with cedar shavings and a soft cloth. For the length of the twenty-minute ride, I worried about his dying. Maybe the ride was too bumpy. (I had put his box on a large pillow and surrounded it with other pillows.) Maybe the truck was too cold. (Probably not; I had warmed it up for ten minutes before putting Harry into it.) On the other hand, maybe this whole thing about a hamster—a creature that most adults wouldn't worry much about, no less drive to a vet—was idiotic. Maybe Harry was just a small-brained animal who lived in a messy cage that stank of urine and was a pain to clean. He wasn't Zoe or me or life.

"Can I see him?" the receptionist asked.

I lifted the lid off the shoebox. The elastic band covering it hadn't been needed. Harry wasn't up to chewing his way out of a flimsy container that couldn't have held him for twenty seconds in his prime.

I was ushered immediately into one of Dr. Grosjean's offices. Dr. Grosjean picked up Harry and gave him a quick examination.

"Would cortisone do anything?" I asked.

"No animal should die without a shot of cortisone?" Dr. Grosjean answered. I wasn't in the mood for irony.

"Can you come back in an hour for him?" he asked.

I objected momentarily. But Dr. Grosjean said he wanted to do everything possible—give Harry a bath to get some scabs off him and make him more comfortable, check for parasites, give him a shot of cortisone. I agreed.

When I got home, Dava had just gotten off the phone. Dr. Grosjean had called to say that Harry was dead. He had died the instant he was put into the bath. Dr. Grosjean was sorry. Should he "take care" of the body or did we want to come back for it? I was too upset to call him back. I thought I would stutter too much. I asked Dava to call and left to get Harry.

The receptionist removed the shoebox from under the counter as I walked in. She handed it to me and said she was sorry. I thanked her and looked inside. "There's a lot of caked blood in his mouth," I said, dismayed by the apparent internal hemorrhaging Harry had suffered. The receptionist said nothing more.

I drove home, crying loudly and raging all the while about the unbearable impotency of being human, my inability to keep a tender part of Zoe's heart alive. And, dammit, I thought, it *hadn't* been so stupid of me to care about Harry. He *was* part of our lives and we a part of his life. And who's to say what kind of life matters most.

A few months back, I had promised Zoe implicitly, silently, from every cell of my recovering being: I'll make things up to you someday. I'll pay you back for the emotional impoverishment and fright of your first five years. I'll keep your pet alive. *I can do that, Zoe; after all, I'm your dad.* I'll even keep myself alive until after you've died of old age. Just stop worrying about death. I can't bear any more of it. I will fill your life with love. Kick immutability in the ass. Make sense of the inexplicable.

When Zoe came home from school a few hours later, she began telling me eagerly about something nice that had happened to her. I waited for her to pause.

I put my hands on her shoulders. "Pooh, I have bad news." Her eyes looked at me as in years before. "Harry died."

Her face contorted. "Harry is dead?"

"Yes, I'm terribly sorry. He's dead."

She came into my arms and wept and gasped against my chest. I held her close. We moved from room to room. Her mom and I took turns being with her. Occasionally I mentioned the past sadnesses in her life. Mostly I just held her.

Isaac and I dug a deep grave. Zoe stayed inside with Dava and drew a beautiful design on a large shoebox. We buried Harry in it, along with his food dish and his favorite treats. All of us put dirt on his grave. I suggested that Zoe form an H on the packed dirt out of small stones. She did. I spoke about a time for life and death and mentioned Harry's good traits. His life had been worthwhile. The wonder and delight and close times his life brought us had meant so much.

We found each other's hands and walked back to the house.

LYING DOWN ON THE JOB

At a time when I had been bedridden for two years, one of the few things keeping me afloat emotionally was my ability to make a living. Without this, I doubt I could have sustained the will to recover.

The question was: *How* to continue making a living from a prone position? An acquaintance told me things could be worse—I should be grateful I wasn't a truckdriver instead of a writer. Small compensation. If I had been a truckdriver, at least my disability insurance would have kicked in. Being a writer, I could draw disability only if I were virtually brain dead. Not exactly a status to shoot for or crow to your friends about. "The good news is I finally *did* get disability. . ."

For the past eight years, since 1973, I had run my own educational direct-mail copywriting and consulting business, working with publishers to market products for use in classrooms. At this moment, though, I was running out of clients and contacts. And although I initially had thought that clients who liked me and had socialized with me would continue sending me jobs, it didn't happen that way. To my sorrow, I had confused friendly business acquaintances with friends.

What work I still had I managed in a physically painstaking fashion. First, I lay on my left side and wrote on a lined pad for about ten minutes until that side became numb. Then, I turned onto my right side and dictated what I had written into a microcassette recorder. A part-time secretary typed a draft and I then proceeded to rewrite in the same manner. What took me an hour then now takes me less than ten minutes on my computer.

Working in this manner, I supported my family by myself from the time Zoe was born until she was two, so that Dava could take time off from work and be with Zoe. During this time, wondering if I might have something wrong with my back that doctors had overlooked, I also undertook a nationwide survey that asked back-sufferers to evaluate different kinds of treatments and practitioners for their particular problems. Just talking to these people was exhilarating, taking me outside my destructive body and making me feel useful if only as a listener. Although there were no medical answers for me from the survey, I remained interested enough to begin organizing and writing about the findings.

At about this time, some six months before Isaac was born, I took one more try at finding medical help for myself, after having seen thirteen prominent specialists to no avail over the previous three years. Luck was with me this time. A brilliant, Harvard-trained young neurologist at State University of New York at Stony Brook ran a series of tests on me and diagnosed my ailment as a rare but not fatal myopathic disorder.

Dr. John Halperin, then Director of the Muscular Dystrophy Clinic at Stony Brook, and now Director of Neurology at North Shore Hospital on Long Island, did something else life-extending for me: He talked to me and gave me hope. That meant at least as much to me as the medications we tried.

Until I got Dr. Halperin's diagnosis, I hadn't really expected to live long. Hence my one goal for the research on back care was to make it into a pamphlet I could give away to people who requested it from ads I would run. (That has a somewhat "noble" sound now, in writing about it, that I assuredly didn't feel then.) In the state of mind I had been in, I hoped the pamphlet would be proof I had done something more with my life than writing direct mail.

In spite of myself, it seemed, the planned pamphlet grew into a book-length manuscript that was signed up by a publisher and later by a book club. Dava, who had been concerned that the project was a "morbid preoccupation with illness," read my manuscript, liked it, and joined me as coauthor in case the book needed someone physically able to travel on a publicity tour.

In April 1984, a month before Isaac was born, and with new medication from Dr. Halperin starting to put some oomph into my physical recovery, I started to plan my first business trip in more than three years.

I wasn't ready to travel, not by normal means anyway. I couldn't sit or stand nearly long enough for a typical business luncheon or meeting. But picturing the unborn Isaac exhorting me to move faster, I decided to try.

If you've ever had a dream about being unable to avoid a relentlessly oncoming terror, you'll understand what I dreaded most about my planned trip. It was, as with the dream, paralysis—literally, my muscles seizing and much of my body refusing to move. This had happened to me twice recently, forcing me to lie where I landed after a fall.

Both incidents occurred during cold weather, which still is the most difficult time for me. The first time, my walking gait abruptly slowed as if pistons in my hips were running low on oil, then running on rust, then frozen still. I stopped, fell, and slithered on my side along the road for a while in an effort to get up.

Another time, while walking along the beach in an area unfrequented except during the summer, I fell and had great difficulty—growing colder and more panicky as the clock in my mind wound down with the dropping temperature—determining how to move to stop the cramping and pain without causing new areas to lose function. I lay there long minutes. My right foot was frostbitten when I got home.

I found myself wondering now if this *really* had happened to me. I wanted to believe my memory might be overly dramatic. I promised myself to try and lighten up and just be damn sure not to fall at the client's.

I pictured how I would walk when I got to the meeting. If the office floors were carpeted, that would make me unusually prone to tripping, so I would have to lift my feet more than usual. Since my legs, especially my braced right leg, tended to not raise easily, I would have to focus well on what I was doing. I made a mental note about how to deal with my forearm crutch at the meeting. I would walk with it gripped in my left hand, with my left forearm positioned in the contraption's adjustable metal clasp. My tendency when I shook hands was to drop my left arm at my side, causing the crutch to slide off my forearm and wrist in the direction of the person I was greeting. I had to remember to tighten the clasp after widening it to accommodate my sport jacket. No sight gags allowed at this meeting. No "hey, sorry, did that crutch clip you in the chin?"

Of course, the scariest thought of all wasn't of falling or KO'ing clients with a forearm crutch. It was my constant fear of relapsing. Losing the progress I had struggled for years to make. Being completely bedridden again when Isaac was born. Repeating the nightmare with Zoe. The unthinkable, which I couldn't stop thinking about.

On the positive side, I would be seeing Maddy Weinstein and that would reduce the pressure of a first trip. Maddy was a friend as well as a client. She knew my medical problems. Before I became ill, she had confided in me about personal matters in her life. More recently, she and her family had visited our home.

The company she worked for, Merrill Lynch, didn't have a project for me at the moment, but that was just as well. I needed a chance to start showing people I was functioning again. Looking for work by phone was disheartening. When you run your own business and are ill for a while, business people don't see you so much as sick as unsuccessful. On top of that, especially if your prognosis is uncertain, your illness pushes people into taking a discomforting blink at their own mortality. All told, I wasn't exactly the guy everyone wanted to work with.

I *had* been able to see clients even after I became ill when we lived in Manhattan, because some clients were willing to come up to my apartment. Our move to East Hampton in early 1982, after Zoe was born, put me some three hours away from most of my business sources. Relocating also removed other kinds of independence I had enjoyed—especially getting food delivered and being able to invite over friends.

Still, I didn't argue long with Dava about making the move, conflicted by ambivalence and guilt as I was—living in a kind of low-grade chronic shock. I wanted to please, to do right by my family. Dava was raising a baby I initially had wanted more than she. Trust me, I had said. Then I had abandoned her to that baby and to her worst fears by becoming ill.

I prepared to move, but with the feeling that my life was someone else's. I had been a jogger, decent tennis player, hiker, driver, person of the world. I was none of those things now. I was an invalid. One who might die from his illness.

Now, two and a half years and a battery of medical tests later, with a prognosis that offered some hope, expecting a second child, I was picking a date for my first trip back to Manhattan, a Monday because it was our postman's day off and he had agreed to drive me.

The ensuing week saw me give a creative, new dimension to the word *obsess*. Even I had to laugh at some of the life-defying pitfalls I dreamed up.

What if my pain became so great at the meeting that I fainted and landed on Maddy? What if she mentioned how frail and tremulous I looked and told me to go home? How *did* I look? What if my old stuttering problem worsened so badly in the lobby of Merrill Lynch or with Maddy's receptionist that I couldn't say who I had come to see?

The backseat of our station wagon, in its reclined position, formed an incline where my head rested. What if that incline worsened my condition on a long trip and I couldn't move my neck?

What if a policeman arrested my driver for stopping in a No Stopping zone when he dropped me off in the crowded Wall Street area? Or arrested me for lying on a mattress without a seat belt? Or arrested me just for looking so damn *weird*?

My postman driver, who was somewhat afraid of Manhattan as some natives of my town are, might get lost while circling the block. What would I do if he wasn't there when I got out? I pictured myself trying to look composed while lying on a Wall Street sidewalk. What if the police assumed I was drunk or crazy and carted me off?

I worried that my brother-in-law, who had agreed to meet me out front of Merrill Lynch with a takeout lunch for me and Maddy, wouldn't be there. (Maddy, surprisingly, had accepted my offer to bring lunch, which gave me confidence that I at least still could sound fine on the phone.)

My meeting with Maddy went well. She greeted me warmly and said I looked good. (She was being generous; I weighed 110 pounds at the time, down from my pre-illness weight of 135 pounds.) I ate my turkey sandwich and coleslaw standing, sitting only for the five minutes I could tolerate toward the end of the meeting. Maddy had no work for me at the moment. A week later, though, one of her managers called with a substantial editing project. The trip had paid off!

I recall having once commented to the wife of a paraplegic I worked with how well dressed and healthy he always looked. "You ought to see what it's like getting him on and off the toilet, not to mention cleaning and dressing him," she had replied bitterly. I often thought of this man when I was at business meetings in the months and years to come, standing, willing casual and unpained expressions, looking freakishly different, acting as normal as I could, an ugly duckling out of place who couldn't swim. If people knew my dirty, little secrets, sniffed them out beneath my layers of freshly pressed clothes and resonant tones, I would be out of business.

These meetings during the first two years of my recovery were bizarre races against time, entailing imaginative efforts to lie about what was wrong with me. Basically I told clients I would have to leave in about an hour "because I have a minor nerve impingement that makes one leg go numb if I sit or stand too long . . . but I'm completely recovered except for that little annoyance."

I smiled a lot at these meetings and told irreverent jokes. People bought this stand-up writer act. When my allotted time ran out, I would walk out of conference rooms as briskly as my forearm crutch and cramping muscles would allow, hoping that last-minute conversations at elevators wouldn't linger.

I usually could find reasons to discourage clients from accompanying me down the elevator and outside. I didn't want them to see me struggling to get into my station wagon—which I replaced two years later with a full-size van, complete with tinted windows that let me disappear from view.

I don't know why I waited so long, money aside, to get a van. Lying in the back of the station wagon, in open view, scorched and drenched in warm weather, felt uncomfortable and even funereal.

Depending on traffic, my driver and I would make our first stop in about two hours at a Howard Johnson's. One driver, let's call him John, always wanted to sit at a table there, instead of at the counter where I would have been able to stand or slouch against the stool seat. John had been a middle-management postal administrator before he retired, working his way up from postal truckdriver. He repeatedly made it clear to me, though not in these words, that eating at a counter was inappropriate for a man of his status.

I always replied in a mumble—something about, well, maybe the counter would be better for me. Then listened to John's silence. And gave in. Off we would go to a table, where John would sit so well ensconced he seemingly became part of the chair, grinningly oblivious to my discomfort at standing. I would stand until the food came, then sit and eat as quickly as I could, spilling food on myself because I couldn't bend over the plate.

DAD AND SON

John would devour my quotables and remarks to feast on later with his wife. "That Art, he's really a card," I overheard him telling her when we stopped once at his house for a moment after a trip. "Wait till I tell you about *this* one . . ."

It was during these years of being driven around, before I got my specially designed truck and could drive myself, in 1988, that I invented the $600 business lunch. I don't recommend it, but there was no other way to get my career moving again. Here's how it worked:

I paid $200 for a driver to make a round trip to and from Manhattan. Then added $50 more for his waiting time during my luncheon meeting, $15 more for his lunch, $15 for parking. I rented a room at a hotel offering room service for lunch, a necessity because I couldn't sit for more than fifteen minutes. A suite was more appropriate than a single room, especially for meetings with a woman client I hadn't met before. The cost of a decent Manhattan suite: $200. The average cost of a room service lunch for two: $75. That's $555 so far. Add $45 for gas, tolls and the driver's dinner on the way home and you've hit the mark.

Of course, that's $600 for a *midtown* Manhattan lunch. In the Wall Street area, it was more expensive and more complicated for me. The official check-in time at the only good hotel in the area was 3 P.M. Checkout was at noon. But I had to stay past noon. Theoretically, then, unless the hotel bent its rules for me and allowed me to check in at noon instead of at 3 P.M. on the day I arrived—or let me stay until 3 P.M. the next day when I arrived the night before—I couldn't take a Wall Street client to lunch. Since my use of a room for lunch couldn't be guaranteed when I made a reservation, the many lunch dates I had at the Vista Hotel, 3 World Trade Center, were preceded by feelings of being the only person in the world with such bizarre problems.

After lunch at these meetings, I would announce as nonchalantly as I could that our meeting would be adjourning to the bedroom. Change of venue, I said. A little medical glitch—a pinched nerve in my leg is acting up. Into the bedroom we would go, where I would lie on my side on the mattress, and with as much dignity and authority as I could muster from this posture, conduct the remainder of the meeting.

Evenings at hotels had their own peculiar complications. I had to bring along a special, condensed-foam foldup mattress I designed for overnight travel; a regular mattress was too soft and made my hips and legs go numb or become overwhelmingly painful. I also traveled with a foldup bedboard, acupressure roller, ice bags and several kinds of medication.

I became frightened late at night when I first began traveling, often lying awake for hours trying to sort out how much of my difficulties might be overcome if only I could will the progress. I was haunted by the idea that something destructive about me was contributing to my physical limitations.

Looking back, if I had to take a guess, I think my progress was a year slower than it might have been. Which in a way is like saying I might have been heavyweight champion if I had been a big guy with a knockout punch. I *would* have had to be someone else. Minimally, I would have needed a totally different internal support system and outlook.

Remarkably, I *was* that totally different person by the summer of 1991. That's when I drove my truck several hundred miles upstate to attend a client's wedding. It wasn't a command performance. I wanted to go. In fact, thinking about the four years I had been driven to meetings, including a monster of a trip with a driver to Chicago, I had *really* wanted to get there under my own power.

To this day, no matter that I ran into painful problems, this journey to my client's wedding best symbolizes for me how far I had come.

The wedding was to be held in the backyard of the groom's parents. To reach it, I had to park my truck in the grass on the shoulder of a narrow country road and walk up an exceptionally long and steep driveway. I debated for an instant whether I should ask someone to drive me to the yard. But I had been making progress of late walking up inclines, and although this climb was my limit or maybe a bit beyond it, I didn't want to pamper myself.

I walked slowly and felt nothing worse than mild tightness when I reached the top. I was wearing a new pair of the same model shoes I always wore. No matter how slowly I tried to break in a different brand of shoe or sneaker, I couldn't do it; I would develop severe hip and leg cramping as well as swelling of both Achilles tendons whenever I tried. The shoes I was wearing on this day were not well broken in yet. I didn't think much about that, though.

I enjoyed the wedding and party afterward, but didn't dance because my hips had become increasingly uncomfortable after I sat for a while. I left while most of the crowd was still partying and drove back to my motel room.

I allowed myself a modest yell of triumph when I got there. I felt good. I had made it to the wedding and was still on my feet. Grabbing a book, I dived onto the mattress. How fine it felt to be able to deal with a plain, old hotel mattress, to be far from home, to be functioning. I felt happier than I could remember.

A few minutes later the toes on my right foot went rigid. I yelled an obscenity and rubbed them as vigorously as I could. In the process my left calf cramped and locked just as badly. I screamed this time. The pain was searing. I started to get off the bed and into my shoes—I can't walk barefoot without bringing on additional cramping—but the toes on my left foot locked downward and held there before I could get my shoe on. I fell back onto the bed.

By lying on my side and experimenting with positions, I was able to keep one of the three cramping areas relaxed. Two cramped muscle groups are hell enough. The vision of a pro football player writhing on the turf with a single muscle cramp flitted through my mind. It was a satisfying vision. I may have been lousy at football but I was good at tolerating leg cramps.

It took two hours for the pain and clenching to subside, leaving me with ten sore toes and one bruised-as-hell calf. I had finally managed to get my anticramping medication about an hour into the episode by taking a header off the bed and crawling a few feet. The extra pill had helped.

I drew a bath and got into it. I had wanted to try a combination of heat and cold during the two hours, but hadn't been able to manage it.

In the tub, feeling relaxed again, I thought how strangely gratifying it was to have an observable and measurable physical symptom like cramping. Sick thought, maybe, but there it was. I had tried to climb a steep hill. I had paid a price. Yet I had stayed away from my gloom and despair of old. I wasn't ill anymore; I had physical problems that I got past at times.

After I eased out of the tub and dried off, I decided to open a window and shout the loudest *I did it!* ever to reverberate around the Catskill Mountains. Certainly the loudest *I did it!* to come out of a motel room with only one inhabitant.

STANDING UP AND DRIVING

Getting back on the road after seven years of being hauled to and fro in a station wagon was the turning point in my recovery from being disabled. Until I could drive again—no matter that my posture behind the wheel was unusual, bordering on downright odd—I didn't realize how much of myself I had lost.

It wasn't the physical places I could now reach that mattered so much. It was the sense that *I* could move on at last. Act on whims. Envision possibilities. Engage a life that seemed my own.

Even stalled in traffic jams I felt celebratory. I am *here*, I would think. This sense of being—not being anywhere in particular—but just *being*, felt like a rebirth. If I had always grimaced snobbishly at the cliché "thrilled to be alive"—I thought it was just fine now. Driving myself places, I felt the rush of expanding flights of wonder and precise moments when life awakens. All this in a 19-foot-long, 9½-foot-high step van that would normally inspire nothing more poetic than the thought of a UPS delivery.

Whirring past exits, or compressed in a Manhattan gridlock, I sang. At the top of my lungs, my tones mingled inevitably as in years past with the fantasy of vocalizing magnificently well. A regular operatic luminary, I. Not really, not close, but who cared? I had sorely missed these private opportunities to burst loose and air out old loves and inchoate passions.

Just to be alone again. That brought tears of wonderment. There was an *I* in the truck underscored by a world flying by outside and by the internal invasions I could now mostly hold in check. No longer the *I* stranded in my bed, turbulently lonely, scored by demons and never at peace enough to feel alone.

99

DAD AND SON

I took to parking on the shores of remote bays and writing poetry in my head or debating with myself about what I saw and felt. I didn't always look at the water. Sometimes I just listened to it, flopped on a comfortable foldup mattress in the back of the truck, head propped on two cozy pillows. You *could* get up and walk on the beach, I told myself. *Sounds good*. Or you *could* just lie here and think. *Fine*. Or take a nap. *Nice idea*. Or cry. *I may need to*. I would smile at what seemed like so many possibilities. For a few precious moments, stretching in time like the hymn of a forgiving angel, I finally felt neither shame nor sorrow that I could no longer run or skate with the kids at the town pond or climb a mountain or walk as fast as my wife. I felt a pulse of life and thought I recognized it as my own. That more than sufficed.

The doubts still came, of course. I sorted through fragmented notions of control and toughness, trying to piece them together and believe in them. I would say, "I'm back." They would argue, "You're still crippled and nowhere." I would try another tack, "I'm getting stronger." They would reply, "Yes, but maybe you made yourself sick; you should be perfectly well now."

Still, the good times were growing. Being a driver again was akin to a magical reappearance. Seeing myself in action for the first time after nearly a decade of invisibility. Having others see me, too. I won praise from any person who had ever stood on a commuter bus or train for an hour or more, when I worked up the nerve to mention I made six-hour round trips to attend business meetings—all done while standing, mind you, meetings included.

I loved and despised the praise I got. Like many people who are chronically disabled, I thought I should be able to do better. Make better use of my mind-body connection, as the media told me to. Imagine health. Will myself to be well. Hook up a cerebrum-to-muscle channel so powerful it cured me. Even made me immortal. And why not? That's the message of hubris we think we hear echoing from ancient Athens: Humans can conquer the forces of nature and the gods; illness, even death, is some-thing one's mind *allows*.

Shortly after I started driving my truck, a friend sent me a satirical newsstand issue called *Standing*. It took a funny poke at the how-to frenzy to learn what people once managed—walking, running, relaxing, even breathing—without a personal trainer. It exhorted: "Nearly six billion people stand every day; if they can do it, you can, too."

STANDING UP AND DRIVING

True. I could stand and drive, too. Pretty good trick. Just don't ask me to *fix* the truck.

I'm very different from most of my male neighbors in my attitude toward vehicles. I drive them. They park theirs next to their hearts. Wax and polish them. Soup and jazz them so baby will hum. I'm talking Strong Man stuff. On your back under the vital parts, greased and smudged for combat, ready and able to lift the front bumper with one palm. No big deal. Just an inherent and fundamental part of a guy's self-acclaimed and self-assured maleness. *Those* guys. Not *this* guy.

When my neighbor's transmission goes, he calls Mr. Unbelievably Mechanical Neighbor—a guy who keeps a spare car in his yard just to strip down and reassemble in case his regular vehicles work well some weekend. Then the two of them go off to hunt the junkyards for a spare transmission that needs some fixing, a complete rebuilding job it turns out, but the price is cheap enough, and they spend Saturday and Sunday, no church, getting her together, the two of them winding up contentedly battered and tired, beers in hand Sunday night, soldiers after battle.

I used to bring my car to a mechanic for an oil and lube. Guys where I live don't do that any more readily than they announce at the annual Memorial Day ceremony that they're into cross-dressing.

Still, at age forty-seven, I would have happily accepted being a mechanical moron if only I could drive. It felt as if going somewhere with my life depended on it.

I had no idea how to proceed.

I think of standing and driving one of the old milk trucks or bread trucks from my childhood, then dismiss the idea. No one drives like that anymore. And seat-belt laws probably make it impossible anyway.

Robby thinks I can drive. He is my psychoanalyst and has been extraordinarily helpful in getting me back into one piece. He is also, however, nearly every bit as daffy as I about the mechanical workings of motor vehicles.

One day, after hearing again from me how pained I am to have to be driven twice a week to the medical building where he works—I feel like a cripple when I get there and hate having to lie to my driver about having to make the trips for extensive dental work—Robby breaks out of his analytical mode and asks me about the possibility of driving standing up.

The thought stays with me, though. Over the next few weeks it evolves into a do-or-die goal. If standing and driving can be done in theory, it can be done by me.

I start looking around.

It quickly becomes apparent there are no trucks in America or Europe designed for drivers to stand without having to use their feet to accelerate and brake.

I take that news in stride; my major hope is to find a step van that can be modified with hand controls and safety belts.

I write to the then U.S. Secretary of Transportation, Elizabeth Dole, explaining my predicament and idea. She responds immediately with a warm and informative letter, referring me to her assistant in charge of transportation for the handicapped. His letter reaches me a week later, assuring me it is my legal right to drive myself for employment purposes and that every effort will be made to help me.

I'm astonished and buoyed by this cooperation.

I write to the New York State Commissioner of Motor Vehicles. She, too, is encouraging and puts me in touch with the Principal Motor Vehicle Inspector of my county, a compassionate soul named James Screeney.

Mr. Screeney is where the buck stops. He is the man I will have to satisfy with my vehicle and with my driving skills. I meet with him and his boss. They put me through simple range-of-motion and muscle-strength tests, which I pass. They also ask me a lot of relevant questions, some of which fill me with apprehension, especially, "Will you be able to secure yourself in one place, standing, while maintaining full control of the vehicle?"

Neither of them knows anyone who drives, or who has ever driven, standing up.

For the most part, though, I feel optimistic. I'm not alone anymore. Now that I understand myself and my needs better, it seems other people do, too.

There is one monster catch: *I can't be tested in theory; I have to get a step van, have it modified and prove I can drive it safely.* If I fail the test, the vehicle is still mine. I just won't be able to drive it legally.

The biggest logistical obstacle has to do with safety belts. New York State law says people can be exempt from having to wear them for a number of reasons, ranging from being short to being pregnant to having phobias about confinement. My situation is not covered. Mr. Screeney urges me to give myself the maximum chance of passing the test by figuring out a way to strap myself into the vehicle. If I'm not belted in, he fears I won't be able to maintain a stable position while turning and braking.

My niece's boyfriend, who has grown up driving trucks of every description on a farm in Iowa, volunteers to drive me around to used-truck lots.

A used vehicle seems best. I'm strapped for money and I can't justify borrowing the price of a new van because it's doubtful I'll ever be able to travel long distances. Taking a guess, I hope I can hold up for an hour tops before the sway of the truck causes my hips and legs to shut down. That might be overly optimistic. There also is the possibility that my legs won't be able to handle the effort required to stand in a moving vehicle.

My outings to used-truck lots prove futile. The step vans with bodies made of steel are rusted to the sky; the aluminum ones have engines driven into the ground.

Worse, I'm beginning to think there is another problem I won't be able to overcome.

When I stand next to the driver's seat in these step vans, I'm positioned too high up, even though I'm only five-feet seven-inches tall, to see out the top portion of the windows. I can see the road ahead but not the traffic lights overhead.

Driving is for the able-bodied and the normally handicapped, not for freaks. Six months after I was inspired to think I could drive myself around, the idea of standing and driving seems unworkable.

I want to quit trying. But quitting means emotionally dying, and I know it.

A few weeks later, I begin searching the classified ads for step vans. I call prospective sellers, specifically to ask a question that tends to baffle them: "When you stand next to your driver's seat, can you see out the top part of the window?" Although I explain as best I can my reason for asking, some people hang up on me.

I finally reach a man who has a truck that sounds promising. While I hold on, he runs out to his driveway, stands next to his driver's seat, dashes back in and tells me he *can* see out the top of the window. I'm ecstatic. That same day I get a ride to his house to check it out.

The van in question is battered looking. I hardly mind. I get into it and stand next to the steering wheel. Stooping just a bit, I have the visibility I need.

However, when I sit to take a short test drive, I find that the truck has neither power steering nor power brakes. In my excitement, I had forgotten to ask about these features. My right leg shakes so violently when I try to apply the brakes that the prospective seller has to clamber onto my lap and bring the van to a halt for me.

The test drive is over.

We discuss my buying the van and having it outfitted with power brakes and steering. But although the man urgently needs the money, he advises me that the frame of the van isn't in good enough condition to modify.

I continue making calls and asking around. I learn there are service centers that specialize in customizing vans and immediately call two of them. The technical experts I speak to are disbelieving. "You want us to help you to drive standing up?" one manager asks. "I can't do that, mister. Do you realize what would happen to me and my business if you got into an accident and killed someone?"

I hire a lawyer, who recommends drawing up a "hold harmless" agreement. I try out this idea on the next conversion center I call. The guy hears me out silently, then says he doesn't do that kind of work.

I go to two garages in my own town, all but begging for help, and get the same reply—no dice, we can't do that.

My condition and this world don't seem to mesh. My search has now gone on for eight months. I am all but resigned to never driving again when my wife suggests I try Gene Simons. She tells me he owns a gas station and body shop in town, has done excellent work on her car and is unusually intelligent and skilled.

"He seems gruff at first," my wife cautions me, "but he's actually a nice guy. I'm sorry I didn't think of him sooner."

I go to Gene's Garage. "You'll have to wait, I'm busy," Gene tells me when I start to explain what I want. He stares at me for a moment, then turns away. I can't read his attitude, but I am horribly self-conscious about my forearm crutch and frail appearance in a world I always have associated with guys tougher than I.

I wait and observe Gene for nearly an hour. We seem an incredible mismatch.

STANDING UP AND DRIVING

Gene isn't gruff, he is beyond that. More a bear with the proverbial thorn in its backside. His phone rings. "Son of a *bitch*," he shouts, kicking a tire rim out of his way before answering, "Gene here," the two words elongated into a statement of capitulation, the doom of being eternally bothered by the whole world at the wrong time.

I'm terrified of this guy, I think. His stature alone is intimidating. Gene Simons may have been tall and slender in a previous life. But he appears now as if glacial action has reconfigured and compressed him into a short, mighty mountain, about my height, but with the girth of two strong men combined.

On the other hand, I note with relief toward the end of my wait that Gene is unfailingly kind, instructive and polite with his employees. They seem to like him. They're hardly intimidated. When one mechanic mentions casually to Gene that he has done something incorrectly and will need more time than planned to fix it, Gene pats him on the shoulder and tells him not to worry about it.

After the last of his half-dozen employees has left for the day, Gene walks toward me. "It hasn't been exactly a good day," he says, mixing vehemence and resignation into a slowly intoned epitaph. He offers me a wry smile. "What can I do for you?"

We wind up talking for an hour and a half. And I wind up liking Gene Simons. He is honorable. And he seems decent and sensitive in a way that more than balances out stories I have heard of his rampaging anger, including tales of his bodily removing irksome customers from his premises. (These stories, I am relieved to learn, are part of local folklore about a much younger Gene; months later he verifies the folklore matter-of-factly, adding with a grin, "I try not to do those things anymore.")

Gene and I make a plan. Since used step vans are in such questionable shape, I won't continue trying to find one. I will buy a new aluminum step van and Gene will do his best to modify it to my needs. I will figure a way to borrow the $20,000 needed. This seems like my best and probably last chance to drive again.

Gene lays down some rules before I leave: "Don't ask me how I'm going to do the job. Don't ask me what happens if I can't do it. Or how much it will cost. I don't know those things. Also, don't ask me when the job will be ready. I'll be able to get to it only on weekends, and then if I'm lucky. But I'll do this for you; we'll figure something out."

———————

DAD AND SON

He had a few final words to say to me at this first meeting. And the memory of those words reminds me more than anything about the essence of the man. Gene was looking down and around when he spoke them, mostly avoiding my eyes. Just as well because I had to fight back tears. "It seems to me," he said, "that if a person like you is willing to try so hard to get well, so he can drive his kids around and get himself to meetings and support his family, I should at least be willing to help."

I bought a truck a week later and had a driver bring it and me to Gene's Garage.

Gene and I talked for two hours more that day. It became clearer to me what had motivated him, compassion aside, to take on a dubious project with no known guidelines and a number of imposing legal uncertainties.

Gene Simons despised the humdrum. And dreaded becoming it. Another brake job, another grease and lube. The routine of his work mocked his talents. "Any grease monkey can do this stuff," he commented at one point. It wasn't that he felt too good for any job. He often took on the most menial tasks, floor sweeping included, rather than ask his workers to. But he welcomed a challenge. He needed the unknown, the seemingly undoable, the jobs as uncommon as he was.

He spoke more explicitly about this the next time we met. I was explaining why I liked to write, how writing was one of the relatively few jobs without a cookie-cutter outcome.

"I know what you're saying," Gene spat. He sized up the truck for a minute. "Most of the work that will go into this will be mental," he said. "That's the job really. A lot of other people could do the mechanical work.

"You're a writer," Gene added. "You could say this project is my novel, getting an idea and seeing where you can take it."

A masterpiece of a novel, it turned out.

When Gene's work was finished—with help from his astute and imaginative friend, Danny Talmadge—Big Blue Truck had a lowered floor area where I could stand and drive at the precise height I would be at if I sat; a front seat I could either sit in or turn around and lean against; a single hand control I could raise up for accelerating and push down for braking; wooden flooring; wall and ceiling insulation; paneling; a unique-in-this-world five-section safety belt made from racing-car belts; an arrangement of iron poles that anchored the safety belts and, incidentally,

---

provided my kids with a chinning bar and traveling playground; a school-bus seat for Zoe and Isaac situated where I could keep an eye on them; and even a concealed antitheft button I could push from inside the truck to turn off the gas pump when I parked in Manhattan.

To accomplish all this took five months of Gene's time. I doubt that turning a car into a speedboat would have been more challenging. Myriad changes were contemplated and abandoned. Several experiments were undertaken, then undone. Over the next two years, dozens more refinements were made to give the truck an even smoother, safer ride.

Gene and I have been friends for five years now. I'm not certain what our friendship meant to him at the outset, but as I struggled to get well and see myself as a man again, it helped me imagine a future. It gave me hope.

The two of us have talked a lot over the years. Ironically, though, until this moment, I never realized how much we discussed the subject of this book.

One day when Gene was talking about trying to give customers the best work he could at a fair price, he said to me, "You have to be a man about what you do; you have to be moral."

This effort to be moral—which necessarily involves having thoughts and feelings about your effect on others—defines for me as well as anything else what it means to be male and human. For Gene, I know the definition encompasses having the humanity to respect each person he deals with, unless that person gives him reason not to. (In which case, duck.) I see him do this with everyone who walks into his place. No exceptions.

He and I get along without the combativeness men often show toward each other—the Keep Out bane of male relationships. We don't share all aspects of our personal lives, but we trust each other's character. Our friendship is rooted there.

We have shared an exciting journey into the unknown—soaring over skepticism, different backgrounds, an absence of guidelines and a host of legal obstacles. We have forged a friendship and, almost incidentally it sometimes seems, we have created in the process the world's only known stand-up-and-drive vehicle.

Thanks, Gene. For the freedom and friendship. For enabling me to shape and live a dream. For getting us into the *Guinness Book of Records* whether Mr. Guinness knows it or not. For giving the naysayers something unpleasant to chomp on. And for helping me to live my life. Standing. Moving again.

THE DRIVING TEST

Trying to anticipate what my stand-up driving test would be like brought back memories of taking three Army induction physicals twenty-five years earlier.

As if one physical wasn't enough, no sooner had the Army collected evidence of my potential fitness as a fighting machine than they lost my records. Two months later, they lost the results of my second physical. During the third physical, when there was an unexplained, three-hour delay, a platoon worth of us stood around discussing the nuances of declaring oneself homosexual, mentally ill, asthmatic or flat-footed.

With my driving test coming up, I felt a similar unreality and lack of control over outcomes.

Toward the end of that third Army physical, we had to take off all our clothing and parade around with our shoes tied around our necks. I doubt this was meant as a taste of harassments to come; more likely it was a military version of tying mittens to sleeves so they wouldn't get lost.

Remembering this strange procedure, which reached its climax when about 150 of us had to toe a long line and bend over for a flashlight-lit anal inspection—presenting the mooning Prostatettes for your viewing pleasure—I couldn't help but muse that I soon would be again in an awkward position.

The idea of taking a driving test standing was not only strange, it was all but unbelievable to me. I hadn't fully accepted being handicapped. On some level I expected to think a magical thought and be fine again.

The Army physicals and the upcoming driving test raised the same question: Was I acceptable in the eyes of others?

DAD AND SON

Both tests conjured up a lifetime of wondering about being adult. I still couldn't define that word for myself. But the authorities judging me could and would. Yup, you're okay. An adult. Nope, you come up short.

Screw being judged by an authority. I tried to convince myself that *I* could be the sole arbiter of my readiness. My truck soon would be ready to drive. If the bureaucrats said I couldn't drive, and I felt I could, I would drive. If I ran into problems with the law, I would deal with the consequences.

Nice fantasy, but one that made my stomach turn on me. Would I really have the courage to drive without permission?

I pictured my first and final illegal ride. Minor accident or traffic violation. State trooper—hat, shades, boots, high-gloss intimidation—approaches me. "Let me see your license," he barks, his voice making James Earl Jones sound like Pee Wee Herman. He peers in the window.

"Jesus, are you driving this thing standing up?"

"Yes, officer," I stutter. "You see, I'm entitled to a life, too, and . . ."

"What the hell's the matter with you, can't you talk? Are you a mental case?" He takes a closer look. "You must be drunk or on drugs." He pulls out his pistol to protect himself and the world from this unlicensed stand-up menace.

Back in real life, the major mechanical roadblock to my being able to take the driving test remained unresolved. The floor area near the steering wheel had to be lowered—without weakening the structure or interfering with the vital goings-on underneath—in order to give me full visibility.

After a few discouraging tries, Gene and Danny devised the perfect solution. They removed a section of flooring, about two feet square, thereby extending the driver's initial step-in level to the steering wheel and slightly beyond, at which point the modified floor stepped back up eight inches to its original height.

The plan for a lowered floor meant that Gene would have to do some adjusting below it. He also would have to cut and weld metal in an exacting manner. My safety depended on it. If the procedure wasn't done exactly right, the bottom literally could fall out. Gene, an expert and enthusiastic metal craftsman, was the right man for the job. As it turned out, the end result looked so good that only another professional could tell that the truck hadn't been manufactured that way.

I called Mr. Screeney at the Motor Vehicle Bureau and made an appointment to be tested in two weeks. That gave Gene and Danny eleven days to figure out and install the hand controls and safety belts. It also gave me three days to find out whether I could physically manage the driving, and if I could, to get in some practice time.

The situation was incredibly fraught. Most other nondrivers have options like taxis, buses and planes. Since I couldn't sit for more than fifteen minutes at a time, I was much more limited.

It seemed as if the rest of my life depended on my passing the test, and I did everything I could think of to get myself in shape for it. For the past three months, to strengthen my arms, I had worked my way up to one hundred curls a day with five-pound weights. I wanted to add more weight—when I was younger I had done four sets of ten curls with a hundred pounds. But now adding even a bit more weight caused my biceps to seize up and stop functioning.

I also had been walking two miles a day, trying to develop an even gait despite my leg brace and forearm crutch. The smoother stride I was able to learn cut down on hip and leg pain. The walking also bolstered my confidence about standing my ground in a moving truck.

More than not, I believed I would drive again. Gene was working miracles with the truck and keeping my spirits high. Suffolk County, where I lived, was willing to test me. I was in slightly better physical condition than I had expected to be.

Yet when people asked me whether I was nervous about the test, I wasn't sure what to say. The years of uncertainty about whether I would live, the doubts about whether I would ever get out of bed and function, had changed me in ways I was just learning about.

I tried to devise strategies to help myself drive longer distances. I could carry along a plug-in ice chest, for example—drive for half an hour, rest and ice down. I could take extra medication on days I traveled. Exercise on rest breaks. Meditate. Whatever I needed to do to stretch my limits.

Gene called me two days later. "The truck's ready for you to try out," he said. "Come on over."

He was still in the truck, making last-minute adjustments, when I got there. I climbed in and stood behind the wheel. Danny joined us and he and Gene instructed me methodically about how to get myself hooked into the five-part safety belt arrangement. I did it incorrectly on the first try, my confusion about anything spatial or mechanical getting the better of me. After they led me through each step several more times, though, I finally got the hang of it.

The process is easy enough. Starting with my left side, I drape one belt over my left shoulder and hook that to a second belt at waist level. Then I link both these belts to a third belt snaking out from under my crotch. Finally, while grasping these three belts at my waist, I join them with shoulder and waist belts from my right side.

Snapped together like this, I was one steadfast driver, all but having relations with the steering wheel.

Gene pulled the truck out of the bay area and positioned it in front of his service station. "It's all yours," he said. "Just go easy when you raise the hand control." He turned around quickly and walked back to his office.

I got in, belted up and turned my head to the rear to check oncoming traffic. I could see nothing but the inside of my truck. Just being able to see out of the truck was going to take getting used to.

I checked my left side mirror, lifted the hand control and sent gravel flying into Gene's gas pumps as I spun out of the station.

Embarrassed but under way.

Five minutes later I was back. The physical effort required to drive the truck was causing me to shake and experience muscle fibrillations resembling world-record tics. But I had done it. I had driven my truck. I felt exultant, flying, raving, new.

I walked into Gene's office. He was doing paperwork. He kept his eyes on it for a few seconds. "How'd it go?" he asked.

Hell, I could sound nonchalant, too. "The truck works real well," I replied. It had worked real well. It was a miracle on wheels with a driver determined to keep the miracle going.

Three days later, after building up to a half-hour of driving and a feeling I could handle the truck adequately if neither my forearms nor my hips quit on me, I was en route to my driving test. Since the trip there would take an hour, I had turned the driver's seat around to its normal position and had John, one of my regular drivers, take me.

I lay on a mattress in the back. We drove in silence for ten minutes. "How do you like the way it drives?" I asked.

"Do you really want to know?"

"Sure."

THE DRIVING TEST

"It's a truck. Bumpy and jarring compared to your Ford wagon. I don't want to discourage you, but I think you're going to have problems driving this thing. It's meant more for cargo than comfort."

Honesty is not only cruel sometimes, it's fucking imbecilic. For the next three-quarters of an hour, I tried to hang in with my choice, spurred on by all the efforts of the past year. John had spent years driving trucks. His judgment might be right. Certainly, if a normal driver, sitting, was uncomfortable, I might be kidding myself to think I could manage more than short trips, if that.

Suddenly something kicked up at me, left me breathless and frightened. I got up on my knees and looked out the window. I could barely distinguish one object whizzing by from the next. My vision had deteriorated badly over the past month. I wasn't sure I could see well enough to take the test.

Talk about repression! How could I have done this to myself? A week from now I would have surgery on my worst eye, which would in all probability be restored to excellent vision. Why hadn't I postponed the test?

A month before, with almost no warning at all, my neuromuscular disorder had brought on abruptly thickening cataracts. Before that, for several years, the problem had been significant but I had let it go unattended—there seemed so little at stake. At this moment I was legally blind in one eye and, if there was a lot of glare or haze, legally blind, period.

A week after my scheduled driving test, when the first cataract was removed, my ophthalmologist, an internationally renowned expert, reported it to be denser than any he had ever seen.

John turned right into the Motor Vehicle Bureau parking lot. I was terrified. Can you try to hide something like this from yourself and still be in any way rational? I took a deep breath. My attitude toward medical problems had been changed radically by my incapacitation. Now if an ailment didn't threaten my life—better yet, if it were a precisely known and easily corrected problem—I put it aside. During the past few years, I had dismissed rotting and infected teeth as sinus headaches. Walked without a crutch immediately after surgery on my knee and Achilles tendon. Taken care of my kids alone for two days while dealing with a raging fever and painful muscles caused by the acute onset of Lyme disease. It wasn't courage, mind you. More an unwitting but practiced ability to shift focus.

I got out of the truck. Mr. Screeney was waiting for me on the back road designated for testing.

He greeted me cordially, promptly crawled under the truck and stayed there for a few minutes. He emerged looking pleased. Then he climbed into the truck and scrutinized everything carefully, all the while talking about his experiences years ago maintaining an Army truck convoy.

He marveled at Gene's work. "Extraordinary job," he said. "Let's take a drive now."

The five racing-car safety belts, attached to poles that could have restrained a bull at the starting gate, awed him. The "fifth belt," the one I wore under my crotch, reminded me of the old joke about an instant tenor waiting to happen.

I lifted the hand control ever so gently. It was a good start. I sensed Mr. Screeney rooting for me.

I felt fine for the first few minutes and ignored the minor tightening in my arms and legs. Then, without warning, my relative calm left. My hands trembled. I worried I might faint.

"Make a left at the blinking light," Mr. Screeney said.

I switched on my blinker, releasing my left hand from the wheel to do so. With my right hand gripping the hand control, I was committing the ultimate driving sin, if only for a second—no hands, Mom.

Mr. Screeney had been watching closely. He asked me to pull over. Calmly he talked me through a way to keep my left palm on the wheel at all times, yet still be able to signal. He also showed me how to keep my hand on the wheel so I could return it to its original position after making a turn.

I eased back onto the road. The sun had come out from behind the clouds. I couldn't avoid its glare, which reflected off my cataracts in a way that whited out details and sketched in a vast, hazy landscape of sameness.

I never saw the blinking light Mr. Screeney had mentioned.

"Coming up soon," he said in a loud voice.

I turned left into a cornfield. What I thought was a blinking light may well have been a passing crow.

End of test, I thought.

———————

THE DRIVING TEST

"You're nervous," Mr. Screeney said. "Let's try it again."

He checked traffic for me while I backed out onto the road. Almost miraculously, the sun vanished behind a cloud. The rest of the test—thirty-five minutes of driving on local roads and highways, through villages, making turns and parallel parking—went well.

Mr. Screeney gave me the word. I had passed.

I parked the truck in front of the Motor Vehicle building. James Screeney, my built-in reason now to forgive all bureaucratic transgressions for the rest of my life, gave me a light pat on the shoulder as we left the truck.

He chatted quietly with one of the clerks. A temporary license was issued to me moments later. It included every restriction imaginable, from hand controls to automatic transmission, corrective lenses to hearing aid.

Badges of honor all. I was a driver again.

Just a few minutes earlier, when I had completed the test and was driving Mr. Screeney and myself back to the Motor Vehicle Bureau, he had asked me what I did for a living. I had mentioned a back book I had written and he had shown interest. Now, wanting to think of some tangible way to express my gratitude, I said I would be happy to mail him a copy of the book.

"Thanks, but we aren't allowed to accept gifts of any kind," he said. He volunteered to buy the book and asked me for details about it.

I tried again. "May I send you one of the copies I got free from my publisher?"

"I appreciate your thoughtfulness," Mr. Screeney replied. "And I wish I could be gracious enough to accept, but there are rules about gifts I feel I must follow."

I thanked him again and made a note to send him a card of gratitude every Christmas. I also promised myself to try being as gracious and decent as James Screeney from this day forward.

I walked back to the truck and turned around the seat for John. We headed for home. I lay on the mattress in back all but bursting with happiness. If I had been alone, I think I could have simultaneously laughed and cried away much of the last seven years of dependency.

I shared the extraordinary news with my wife when I got home. Then drove to Gene's gas station.

Gene beamed with pleasure. We shook hands. I gave him all the details of Mr. Screeney's glowing reactions to the truck's modifications. The few details I forgot, Gene remembered to ask about.

What to say to this man? "Thank you, Gene," I said. I run out of words at the most feeling times of my life. Maybe we all do. We're leveled to phrases of honesty without pause or cleverness or eloquence. "I love you," I told my wife when I married her. "God, how beautiful," I said when Zoe and Isaac were born. "I'm so sorry," I told my best friend when he informed me he was dying.

"Well, you did it," Gene said.

It was true. I really did it. I really fucking did it!

I drove home singing—bass/baritone even with the crotch belt—vocalizing to rattle the roof.

A TRIP WITH MY DAD

My dad and I made our first pleasure trip together late in our lives. In the fall of 1991, we went to the Baseball Hall of Fame. Dad was eighty-four at the time. I was fifty-one.

We may make other trips down the road. But, for me, none will crown this long-overdue journey to our hearts and to the remembrance of sounds that orchestrated our best times together—the balmy cadence of bat hitting ball, ball thudding mitt, boy nestling in dad's lap at least in the boy's wishes, listening to New York Giants baseball on radio—as close to a symphony of snuggles as Dad and I were able to play some four and a half decades ago.

My dad was as thrilled as I about our trip. Surprisingly, I feel no presumption about making this judgment. For on our trip to Cooperstown I discovered that Dad and I knew each other far better than I had thought, usually in ways that lacked even the faintest warnings of recognition until they surfaced. When they did surface, I could no longer remember clearly how distant the journey between our lives once had been.

No other trip I could imagine—this one so plainly made, old shoes strung together after so many disparate journeys—could speak of our love as clearly.

The love had been there ever since when. But Dad could rarely show it and I could rarely feel it. Once on the road, driving along, I realized I never had been alone with my dad this long. Then, almost nonchalantly, the way you realize one day, even though that day is seemingly no different from any other, how well something you treasure has worn years after you acquired it, I understood once and forever the essence of my dad's fine qualities. They weren't what I had yearned for as a child or as a young man. I had wanted, mourned for, raged about, other kinds of goodness, traits more warming than Dad's unassailable integrity, civility, sense of fair play and dedication to public service. But now the lifelong decency and effort of the man held me close. I was loved. This dad was fine with me.

I love my dad. This was the first time I knew it without the wish to understand it. Here we were. Quite an odd couple. Shy with each other in ways; each other's intimate mind reader in other ways. An intimacy based more on memories of what we had meant to each other than on what we had said. At peace finally over who was dad. Each other's dad and son. Sharing the driving in Dad's car because it was more comfortable for him than sitting in my truck. I not minding in the least Dad's chauffeuring me around when I needed to stretch out on the backseat to ease my muscles. Both of us unabashedly happy in the way boys are to be with a favorite playmate.

A few years before, I had cornered my dad in the kitchen one night after dinner when the rest of the family was in the den, and told him it would be nice if we could get together sometime soon for dinner. Just the two of us, I had said. I would be glad to drive to Westchester County and meet at a restaurant near him.

Dad had paused for a few seconds before answering. "Wouldn't it be difficult, given your physical problems, for you to sit in a restaurant?"

I had been able to sit in restaurants for two years, and had done so numerous times with Dad and the rest of the family.

"I'm okay now at restaurants," I said. "It would be nice to see you—you know, just to talk, guys' night out."

There was no visible response.

"Let me know if you want to," I said.

I don't know why Dad didn't take me up on that invitation. Probably he didn't think it would be fair to my mom to go off without her. Or possibly he worried that I would be confrontational about something personal; I had done that several times when I was younger. More likely, he wanted to say yes, to be closer, but without context for articulating that idea.

I hadn't planned to try again getting together with Dad. But the more time I spent taking care of my own kids, the more I found I wanted to spend time with my own dad.

A TRIP WITH MY DAD

So late in the summer of 1991, with summer baseball days slipping away and the Mets playing so poorly that Dad and I could find nothing to express about them but our mutually felt disgust, I gave him a call.

"I have a great idea, Dad," I started my sell. "You and I have talked baseball all of our lives, but we've never been to Cooperstown. How about we drive up there this fall?"

"I've been there," my dad said. "Your mom and I went the first summer after my retirement as school superintendent. It was the first of several summers I taught doctorate-level courses in administration at Cornell. Do you remember that?"

"I remember," I said.

"That's when your mom and I went to the Baseball Hall of Fame," Dad said. "It's quite an interesting place."

"I'd like to go there with you, Dad. We could go on a Saturday and come back the next day."

"We'll think about it," my dad said.

I wasn't sure what that meant. I felt annoyed. "Dad, let me say it again. I want to go to Cooperstown with you," I persisted. "Do you want to go with me?"

"Yes, of course," Dad said.

I suggested alternate weekends in October. Dad said he would get back to me.

When I spoke with my mom a few days later, she said Dad was excited about making the trip with me.

"He hasn't told me which weekend yet," I said. "Let me talk to him."

Dad *was* excited. And so was I. We picked a weekend in October and by the next day he had arranged for a motel room and called AAA for directions.

I was ready for this trip with my dad. But I wasn't equally prepared for the reactions of male friends and acquaintances.

Max, my literary agent, a sensitive and learned man I'm very fond of, and some twenty years my senior, said, "You're very fortunate that your dad is still alive and can make a trip like this." The tone of his words sounded envious to me, almost as if he were angry that I had the dad/son relationship he had wanted. I thought of telling him how difficult it had seemed most of my life to reach my dad. I said nothing, though. Max was right. I *was* fortunate.

DAD AND SON

James, a wonderful new friend, father of three young children and newly bloomed intellectual headed for a master's degree at thirty-five, said flatly in response to my news, "I never really had a father, you know. He left me when I was young."

My friend, Andy, fiercely intelligent and probably the only Marxist alive well versed enough in the nuances of our national pastime to be a hitting instructor, quipped, "Gee, can you take me with you?" It was as close as any male friend came to wishing me a good time.

The night before the trip, after my mom, dad and I devoured my mom's delicious roast chicken dinner, complete with mashed potatoes she bakes rather than boils and magically makes more delectable than anyone else can, we went into the den to talk. The room had been mine when I was a kid. Now there was a pinup calendar on one of the walls of my old built-in pine desk. I got up to take a closer look. "Hey, Dad," I said, "this is pretty sexy stuff."

"It's a calendar from the local dry cleaner," my father said. It would have sizzled the wall if it had been from the local parish, I thought.

"Your dad just finished reading two sexy Danielle Steel novels," Mom said. "I haven't read them."

I looked at my dad, who was relaxing in his favorite TV-watching chair. He winked at me.

"And you don't mind any of this racy stuff, Mom?"

"Not at all," Mom said, "as long as it makes your daddy happy."

Daddy looked happy. He also looked a far cry from the dad who had stonewalled me about the same topic thirty-two years ago.

It had been left to Mom to speak to my sisters and me about sex. She had given each of us a book and tried her best to encourage questions. Dad had ducked the subject entirely . . . until I was twenty, that is, when I insisted on a chat about life with him. What are your views on premarital sex, Dad, I had asked him. Do you *have* any views about sex you want to share? For example, do you think premarital sexual intercourse is okay for a boy but not for a girl? Did *you* have sex before marriage? What would you advise *me* to do?

And that was just for starters. I was relentless. The moment was grim—a gulf between us that threatened to become us.

Dad had been resting on his bed at the time, so I must have interrupted his nap to boot. "You'll feel ashamed the rest of your life if you have intercourse with a woman before marriage," he said after his tyrannical son kept persisting. "And you'll be responsible for making that woman feel dirty for the rest of her life."

I had gotten what I had come for—a reason to keep attacking him. I called him a prude. I explained to him how the world had changed and how women had the right to enjoy sex, too. I lectured him at length, probably wanting him to stop me. I didn't mention that I had striven for little but premarital sex since age thirteen and felt bad that he was implying I was immoral. He didn't tell me anything about himself. I hectored, he scolded. I shut down, he closed up. Our roles were ungiving and unswerving.

Dad and I left for Cooperstown early in the morning, precisely on Dad's schedule. He drove the first sixty-five miles. "I always clock the mileage on trips," he said. I drove the next sixty miles. The accelerator in my dad's new Oldsmobile was easy to touch down with my braced right leg, and I felt that if I iced my leg at the motel that night, I would be okay.

We talked about Mom and my sisters for a while. When it grew quiet for a moment, I mentioned that I had brought along a college-lecture audiocassette series on Shakespeare. Dad had taught high school English and drama before he became principal and superintendent. I thought he would be interested.

"There isn't a cassette player in this car," he said.

"There probably is," I said. "New cars come with one. Maybe you just haven't used it before."

He hadn't. I put the tape in and turned it on. A few seconds later I turned it off because Dad had started talking about his former colleagues back when he first began teaching. At one point he interrupted himself, "You really have me talking nonstop."

I was happy. "Don't pin your being talkative on me," I said. We laughed. As we got closer to Albany, where my dad grew up, he talked about men who had helped his career. When the men had great meaning to him, he gave their middle initials, just as he does today on his answering machine. "This is the home of Louis M. and Miriam B. Klein," the tape begins.

On the outskirts of Albany, Dad told me about a college baseball game he had starred in for Albany State Teachers College. He had been shortstop and captain of the team. That day, he had hit two triples, both of which had landed on an adjoining tennis court. "I was a dead pull hitter," Dad said. "We won that game, 2 to 1. We beat Cortland, I think."

I had been thinking a lot recently about my own impending old age. What would I want to reminisce about with my kids in twenty years? What did I want to do with the time remaining? What mark would I leave? My dad's legacy undoubtedly would be more tangible than mine. He had the Louis M. Klein Middle School named for him, in Harrison, New York. A child-care center. Even a doubles tournament played each year at the New York State superintendent's convention. Someday there would be a street in my hometown named for him, too. I expected and wanted that for Dad.

Whenever I stay at my folks' house, I read and reread a laminated newspaper clipping on a wall of what used to be the den and is now my dad's office. The room is half a flight down from the kitchen and half a flight up from my mom's antique shop, away from regular family activities. I sleep there when I visit. Two of the room's walls are blanketed with certificates and honors. The other two display Dad's sports trophies intermingled with books. The books on one side of the window are mostly collections on famous people—sets on Lincoln and Jefferson, for example, and some biographies I've given Dad over the years. On the other side of the window, there mostly are public-speaking reference works. Dad loves to give speeches. He uses the books to glean jokes and anecdotes appropriate for the occasion. Bennett Cerf, Joey Adams and Sam Levenson are on these shelves.

The front-page headline about Dad from the article I'm inevitably drawn to was published in the local daily newspaper. It reads: "If I could live my life over again, I would live it the same way—Louis M. Klein, Superintendent of Schools, Union Free District 6."

Driving along with Dad, I think mostly of things I wish I had done differently. Then, as though our minds are cohabiting, Dad hurls me back to the present by repeating the newspaper headline verbatim.

"I'm stunned. That must be a lovely feeling, Dad," I tell him. "I'm glad you feel that way."

I glance at him. He looks thoughtful. A moment later, he tells me how he used to earn $8 to $14 a night playing semipro basketball in a neighboring town. "That was more than I made as a teacher," he says. I know the story, but Dad's retelling holds my attention. I'm picturing Dad as a younger man and seeing myself at that age. And trying to reconcile the two images. For most of my life, Dad seemed realms above anything I could be. Now, maybe simply because I saw him as a man as much as a dad, engaging in the common struggle as best he could, I felt as one with him.

I listen only dreamily to further recountings of his hardcourt exploits. But I pay more attention to the reflections that follow. I haven't heard them before.

Dad explains to me that he stopped playing basketball at twenty-six. He felt he had to when he became school principal. "I didn't think it would be right to keep playing," he tells me. "I couldn't be seen doing things that weren't according to Hoyle."

"Like what?" I asked the man I had thought to *be* Hoyle.

"Well, my nickname back then will explain it. Do you know what it was?"

I didn't.

"Hippo," Dad said. "I wasn't a great offensive player [so much for my always thinking him a deadeye shooter], but I was an excellent defensive player whose job it was to guard the other team's top offensive player." He mentioned how the best scorer in the league had played tricks on him early on, stepping on Dad's foot when he was going up for a jump ball (which occurred after every basket then) and tugging on Dad's shorts.

Dad quickly learned to return the same favors to this hotshot—adding tricks of his own, especially using his hips to keep his opponent off balance. The guy stopped fooling with Dad after a few games. "He didn't like having me guard him," Dad said with a smile.

We stop for lunch at a Friendly's. Dad grins at me. "Well, we're doing really fine, aren't we?"

I feel caught off guard for a moment. I assure him we are doing fine, but my voice is tight. Then I realize *I* had wanted to ask that question. I had wanted to be reassured. I return his smile. "The trip is going great, Dad." It is.

Dad had mentioned earlier that he might want to stop at an Albany cemetery to visit the graves of his mother, father and sister. I ask him now if he wants to do that after lunch, and also if he wants to visit his brother Joe, who lives nearby in Schenectady and has recently been ill and troubled by double vision. Dad says no . . . maybe on the way back . . . he is anxious to check in at our motel.

DAD AND SON

I volunteer to pay for lunch, but Dad says the trip is on him. "Your daddy will pay for everything," he says. If I were in a restaurant with my daughter Zoe, age eleven at this writing, and called myself her *daddy*, she would be embarrassed. I am delighted.

Back in the car, I ask Dad if he knows the way to the motel. He says it is outside Cooperstown and that he will drive there and ask for directions.

That seems illogical to me. Besides, I want to prove I can find the way for us. I check the map on the motel brochure. We will pass the motel and drive twenty extra miles if we go into Cooperstown. I tell Dad this.

He agrees to let me drive. When the motel appears where I had predicted, he is pleased. "I'm Louis M. Klein," he says, striding toward the motel manager. "This is my son, Arthur."

When I was little, it used to scare me when Dad got flustered and lost looking for new places. Even more distracting was his wondering aloud halfway through a meal or sports event where he had parked the car. He seldom knew. Whenever we went anywhere that had a parking lot of any size, I hoped my mother or older sister was along to help us find the car.

An hour later, after unpacking and calling home, we set out for Cooperstown. I assure Dad I can follow the local map and get us to the Hall of Fame.

I find a parking space three blocks away from where I figured the Hall to be. After walking a few minutes, I announce there is only one block to go. Dad doesn't respond. I look around. I have been talking to myself; Dad is no longer with me.

I stop and scan the streets and storefronts. Still no Dad. A minute later I spot him walking rapidly out of a souvenir shop. "The Hall of Fame is one more block up, straight ahead," he says. He starts to walk.

"Hey," I say. "Wait. Where'd you go?"

He flashes his broadest Louis M. Klein smile. "I asked for directions."

"Dad, I knew the way," I protest with a cheerful grimace. I had known the way. Which was no small accomplishment. After years of getting lost on every trip I took, I had gotten slightly better at reading maps. Dad looks at me sheepishly. I pat him on the shoulder and we start to walk again.

This is when I first notice that Dad is carrying a brown paper bag with him.

During one of my mom's recent estate sales, at the home of Dr. Tanny, a prominent sports orthopedist, Mom had found and saved a framed black and white photograph. Posing in the photograph were Hall of Famer Ralph Kiner, Bing Crosby (then part owner of the Pittsburgh Pirates), Dr. Tanny and a man we couldn't identify. Dad has brought the photograph with him.

At the head of the ticket line, while people behind us fidget, Dad explains to the young ticket taker that he has a rare photograph he wants displayed on a wall in the Hall of Fame. She is baffled but polite, explaining that neither the curator nor the assistant curator is available, but that Dad might instead talk to the head librarian.

We walk to the library. A lengthy discussion between Dad and the librarian ensues. I can't make out what she is saying, but Dad's voice reaches me wherever I walk on the first floor of the library to look at photos.

A few minutes later, I join Dad at the librarian's desk. It is unlikely the photo will be displayed as Dad wishes, the librarian says. And, no, she can't give him a statement for tax purposes, either. She does, however, promise to put the photo in the library's archives where researchers and the public will have access to it.

Dad seems satisfied. As we are leaving the library, he repeats to me what he told the librarian, "I'm certain they don't have that picture; it's valuable."

After two hours of seeing the sights at the Hall of Fame, Dad mentions the time limit on the meter where I parked his car. I ask him whether he wants to see more of the Hall of Fame or walk back to the car. He chooses the latter.

As we walk, I ask him where he wants to eat dinner. Dad had asked the motel clerk for suggestions and had looked carefully at four menus. But now he says the choice is mine. He sounds testy, tired it turns out, which he readily admits when we sit down at a restaurant I have chosen for its proximity to the car. "We can watch the car from here," I say, seating us near the window.

The sixth game of the World Series between the Minnesota Twins and Atlanta Braves will be on television in two hours. Dad and I had planned to see it together, but when I mention getting back to the motel to see the game, Dad says he is going to retire early. He doesn't want to join me for a swim in the motel's heated indoor pool, either.

I am more worried than disappointed, though I had looked forward to, fully expected, spending the evening with him.

_____

DAD AND SON

When we get back to our rooms, I feel exhausted. I had napped for forty minutes when we first arrived. Now I fall asleep for another hour.

Dad had been through prostate surgery a few months before. I wonder whether the aftermath is still making him tired. His being eighty-four doesn't explain to me why he isn't up for an evening together. At five feet eleven inches and 162 pounds, Dad is lithe and athletic looking. He still plays tennis regularly, bowls nearly every week, chairs meetings at a local bank, runs a guidance service, participates in numerous civic functions and helps my mother with her estate sales.

I wonder how I will feel about death if I live to be Dad's age. He is thirty-three years older than I. I have been flooded with thoughts about my life on this trip. My last thirty-three years suddenly seem like a mindless blip to me. I haven't done enough. It has taken me so long to know myself fairly well. I am not able to say, unlike Dad, that, given the choice, I would live my life over in the same way. I can't say that my name will be granitized for people to see and remember. I feel scared, both about what life will bring and what death will end. I wonder what Dad is feeling.

Early the next morning, Dad knocks on my motel door. He has watched most of the game and feels refreshed after a good night's sleep.

After breakfast at the motel's breakfast room, Dad exits the restaurant door that leads to the pool area. I assume he wants to look at the pool. After a few seconds, he walks into the men's room near the pool then comes right back out. "How do you get out of this place?" he asks.

I show him the way and ask for first dibs at driving home. Dad agrees. After a few moments, he tells me I drive well.

"Thank you, but you're really complimenting yourself," I say. "You taught me well."

"I taught all of you kids," Dad replies.

We are fairly quiet on the way home. I think about the things Dad has taught me. He has lived a life of good-heartedness. He is moral, a model of the kind of civility it takes to keep the world going. He is a gentleman who used to tip his hat to every woman we passed on the streets of our small town. A believer in human rights. An educator who set high and innovative standards. Above all, Dad is—and this is the inscription on a trophy I picture on his office bookshelves—a public servant who had no price.

I recall one of the few times I ever saw Dad with tears in his eyes. He had been outraged, angered beyond words, by a wealthy local man who had offered him a huge bribe to falsify his son's academic records so that the son could get into college. Dad had told the man where to get off. I'll bet anything he did it without using a single swear word.

Dad has taught me well about many things that matter in my life. As I start for home, I look his way. He gives me his broadest Louis M. Klein smile.

LOOKING BACK

BOYHOOD SNAPSHOTS

I recently was watching a New Jersey Nets pregame show on the Sports Channel. The Nets were playing the Utah Jazz and one of the Nets announcers was describing six-foot nine-inch, 260-pound, all-star Jazz power forward, Karl Malone. Nicknamed "The Mailman."

"Now there's a real *man*," the announcer genuflected.

All five feet seven inches and 130 pounds of me reflected: What did that make the rest of us?

This insanity, this bogus "real man" myth that destroys real men, starts early and never ends. By the time Isaac reached second grade, he and his classmates were already evaluating who the toughest kids and best athletes in their class were, which kids could kill you with a karate blow and how lifting weights could build big muscles.

As I watched the opening tip, I wondered whether Karl Malone ever had doubts about being manly. Maybe I could get him and some of his behemoth buddies to go on Geraldo or Oprah and tell all—"Coming up next on *Oprah* . . . Big Men Reveal Humongous Insecurities . . . If you think monster-sized sports stars are never insecure, think again . . . larger-than-life problems land many on shrinks' couches . . ."

In reality, though, it comes to size and muscles, forget sensitivity and liberation. Few males would turn down being hulking giants, just as few women would demur about metamorphosizing into hourglass magnificence.

I had always wanted to be big. As big as a Mack truck. Or minimally as big as Karl Malone. When that didn't happen, I at least wanted to know I loomed big in my dad's eyes. Did he think I was a real man?

DAD AND SON

"Dad, what was I like as a boy?" I asked him one day, tiptoeing toward more important questions.

My father looked at the twenty-year-old before him and paused, looked around the room, then at his shoes. "You were a good boy, a good student," he recalled.

"Yeah, I know, but what was I *like*, Dad?"

My dad looked angry or annoyed. "You were persevering," he said.

I pictured a mule. A rather small mule.

Dad couldn't tell me more.

"Mom," I asked a few days later, "what was I like as a kid. What did I do during a typical day?"

"You read and played," my mom remembered, "and followed me around all day and asked me questions. Like 'Mommy, why do you dust every day if the dust comes back the next day—why not wait for more dust and have fun for a day?' And you were smart, Artie. Years later, I thought about what you had said about cleaning, and after my feet started hurting in my old age I decided to dust less." My mom's recollection, in spite of its lack of heroic dimension, made me feel better about myself.

These days, my sense of being male is relatively comfortable—no gurus or faddish be-all-you-can authorities needed. I have passions and goals, choices, love and friendship. I'm a man, masculine, by definition. I feel like I'm finally starting to fit my own skin.

These are new feelings. Until the past several years, I was more at ease being isolated—no matter how desolate that felt—than I was being open with people. I had been housebound with physical problems. But, more than that, I had spent most of my life as a "housebound male"—a man, like many others, defined and limited by whatever intimacy exists within the walls of the home. Unable or unwilling to build close relationships outside. Surrounded by work and sports buddies, but friendless really. If I *really* needed to talk? I would talk to a woman.

It's easy to forget that males have a good track record for being wonderful friends when they're very young. Little boys make friends with ease. They want playmates. They want to feel close to other boys. They agree on a toy to share, a game to play, and a new friendship is underway. For a few precious years, perhaps only from three to five, we boys don't have to think much about which of us is better. Or whose whatever is bigger. We aren't locked in yet: athlete or klutz, charmer or bore, giant or shrimp, mogul or milquetoast, winner or loser. We're accepting. We can play *Duck, Duck, Goose* without embarrassment. Play tag regardless of foot speed. No one gets left out of games because "he stinks and we don't want him on our team."

I want to remember this kind of sweet, culturized male camaraderie, carry it around with me. Especially when I'm on business trips surrounded by the posturings that keep men alone. Or when I'm isolated by the big-guy mentality of the Nets announcer and his myriad clones. Or on days when I don't feel like much of anything.

I want to hold onto other positive images of what being male can mean. The ones that follow were lived with Isaac. But I believe they fairly portray what we males are like to the extent we're allowed or allow ourselves to be human.

NURTURER

I was going to have knee surgery in the morning. Two months earlier, as well as a year before that, I had been in the hospital for cataract surgery. The kids were asking me a lot of questions, articulated and not, about whether I might become bedridden again.

I told them repeatedly this wasn't a relapse. Just a minor glitch in the knee caused by my old muscle problems, I said. I might have to use crutches for a few days, but I'd be home the same day as the surgery and in no time at all we'd be playing kickball again in the back yard.

I ended my bedtime incantation to Isaac that night with "See you tomorrow" instead of my usual "See you in the morning."

"I want you to say 'See you in the morning,' " he stated in an unbudging tone. "I want you to say goodbye to me in the morning, Dad, before you leave."

I told him I would be leaving at 6 A.M. and didn't want to wake him. We should say goodbye now, then I would be home and see him in the afternoon when he got back from his summer play group.

He burst into tears. He wanted to see me in the morning. His voice and crying grew more insistent. I wavered, uncertain about how best to keep him from worrying. Finally I said I would wake him at six in the morning if he would promise not to be upset and go right back to sleep.

DAD AND SON

It was a dumb promise to request. But Isaac promised and he sounded so grown up I believed him.

A few minutes later, Zoe came back from a planned sleepover at a friend's. She had been too nervous about my surgery to sleep at her friend's. Dava and I were in her bedroom trying to comfort her when Isaac came in. "Your talking woke me," he said, joining us on Zoe's bed. During a lull in the conversation, with Zoe still crying, Isaac knelt beside her on the bed, put his arms around her and held her tightly.

Zoe's smile broke through her clenched memories of a chronically ill dad. The unabashed love of this little nuisance, this "he's-too-weird" embarrassment, this pesty brother of hers, this Isaac person, had made her feel better.

When Isaac got up and went back to bed, Zoe followed him. She fluffed his pillow, straightened his sheets and blanket and kissed him goodnight.

This never had happened before.

At six in the morning, I tiptoed into Isaac's bedroom and kissed him lightly on the cheek. Isaac is usually a deep sleeper and a notoriously grumbly one even when awakened for something exciting he wants to do. I hoped he wouldn't wake up. That way I could say I tried to get out of the house without his being upset and waking Zoe and Dava.

Isaac immediately opened his eyes and grinned at me. "Hi, Dad, are you all set for your knee surgery?"

It felt as if he had magically turned into a dad person by calling into play a mystery mechanism doctors hadn't yet discovered. With each passing year, moments like these would turn into hours until one day Isaac would be an adult. A man. A good man.

"Hi, pooh bear. Yes, I'm leaving now. I'm all set and everything is fine. You go back to sleep now, okay? I'll be here when you get home this afternoon."

"Hey, you," Isaac said, mimicking the way I sometimes talked to him when he tried to refuse me a goodnight kiss. He sat upright, quickly grabbed my head with both his hands and kissed me hard on the lips, godfather style.

Then he lay back down. "Is good luck the right thing to say?" he asked. I nodded.

"Good luck, Dad," he said. "And don't forget your crutches . . ."

He was asleep before I left the room.

134

BOYHOOD SNAPSHOTS

PETER PAN

"I don't want a beard when I grow up," Isaac said. "I'm going to shave mine."

"Fine," I said, and gave him a brief lecture on shaving cream, razors, the perils of nicks and the styptic quality of toilet paper.

"I don't want to shave because I don't want to grow up," Isaac clarified.

"There's no rush," I said. "Don't worry about it."

"I mean I *never* want to grow up," Isaac explained. He had tears in his eyes. "Not ever. Not even when I'm older."

"Why don't you want to grow up?" I asked.

"Only a grown man can tell you that," he answered, twisting and turning until he wound up in a scrunched fetal position on the bed.

I promised he wouldn't have to grow up right now or any time soon. He placed my hand on his cheek and drifted off. A minute later he opened his eyes and closed them again. He did this several times more until he fell asleep deeply.

I went downstairs. He joined me a few minutes later.

This was the third evening in a row he had awakened right after his bedtime after at least a year of getting to sleep quickly and lasting through the night. Tonight Dava and I were ready for him, though. We ordered him back to bed.

Isaac protested, saying that it was cruel to make him spend the night alone without parents. How would *we* like that? We stood firm. As he trudged slowly up the stairs, he turned to us, his face as sad as the world in mourning. "I'm never going to figure out how to live this life as a grownup," he said.

SEXUAL BEING

Isaac made a tent shape of his sheet with his knees. "Guess who's in the tent?" he asked.

I wasn't in the mood for a guessing game. It could be anything or anyone under there—God, a tarantula spider, freaky looking TV creatures whose names I never could remember.

"C'mon, Dad, guess."

"Okay. Batman, Peanuts [our cat], Mommy, a spider, the hamsters."

DAD AND SON

He shook his head.

"I give up," I hastily confessed.

"Mrs. McBride and Mrs. Field . . ."

I stifled a yawn, not thinking at the moment about Isaac's gift for comic timing. Always count to three, silently, before delivering your punchline.

". . . naked."

Blasphemy. His *kindergarten teachers*.

"And I'm naked, too."

"Uh huh."

"No, I mean I really *am* naked."

"That's true."

"Are you going to sleep naked tonight, too, Dad?"

"Yes."

Isaac shifted his knees to make his tent larger. "Now everyone is eating. There is a picnic going on in the tent. They're eating a hotdog and a cheeseburger. They're putting on raincoats, but they're surprised that it doesn't rain, so they take them off and the sun shines. Wasn't that a nice story?"

"Yes, it was very nice."

He pulled the sheet over his head. "Guess where I am."

"Isaac, it's time for sleep."

"Okay, but the picnic made me hungry. Have you ever thought of eating girls, Dad?"

"No," I replied.

"You should try them," Isaac said. "I'd like to eat some girls; they're made of sugar and spice you know, not puppy tails and frogs."

"Pleasant dreams," I said to Isaac.

Good Lord, I said to myself.

EUNUCH

Isaac at age three was walking around the house clutching himself. He had been doing it most of the day, and, for that matter, most of the past month.

"Why are you holding yourself?" I asked.

"I'm making sure it's there," Isaac replied.

"Oh, it's there," I said. "No one can take it away from you. In fact, Isaac, no one ever has lost his penis." A headline flashed into my mind from a trip I made to the grocery store many years ago, where the front page of a lurid tabloid read, "Doctor Accidentally Removes Man's Manhood." I dismissed the memory. "It's yours for life," I reiterated.

A few minutes later, as he was getting into the copilot seat of my truck, Isaac asked, "Has a woman ever had her vagina fall off?"

REJECTED LOVER

Dava was away, and I was facing a job deadline, so Diana Schrage, a lavishly nubile eighteen-year-old neighbor, came over for the second night that week to sit for the kids.

I joined her and them for a quick pizza supper. Isaac was in a lather, whirling in circles around his chair as he talked, mumbling to himself. No one could understand a word he was saying. I was about to launch into my "Sit down and eat your dinner" routine when he came to an abrupt halt.

"Diana," he said, looking febrile and scattered.

Diana stared at him. With her long corkscrew hair flying hither and yon to frame her face in a variety of stunning looks, and one particularly engaging corkscrew flopping over an eye, she mostly looked as if she had whooshed from Woodstock to the '90s without aging.

Isaac hunched his back and paced another circle, Groucho Marx style.

"Diana?"

She continued staring at him.

"Diana, I don't know much French yet, but I want to tell you something. You see," he cleared his throat, "you see, if I talk a certain way it will sound French. Listen." He made a whirring sound, part motor starting up, part cat trying to extricate a furball, finishing it off with what he took to be a French accent. "I love you," he declared, the *youuuu* gravelly and lingering. Not bad for a five-year-old who didn't know any French and had only his Dad's *non*s and *merci*s as grievously bad models.

Diana continued staring.

Isaac probed his memory. I had mentioned a phrase to him and Zoe the night before. "*Je vous aime*," he pronounced.

DAD AND SON

Diana gave a little head flip, shifting her hair and gaze to me. "I took Spanish," she said.

LOVING WARRIOR

When Isaac was two, he was a kinetic contortion of snuggles, kicks, kisses, punches, hugs, gyrations and, most dramatically, sword thrusts. I wasn't physically able to keep up with his movements. But, happily, it seemed more the loving side, less the physical, he needed from me.

Most of his waking hours were spent doing battle. I had forgotten that little boys did that.

One day he began walking around with a gray plastic sword in his diaper. He would whip it out and scream, "By the power of Grayskull, I am He Man." I shouldn't have been taken in by such primal boy-warrior behavior. But I was. I was completely dazzled and enchanted. I asked Isaac to perform his macho-baby act for grandparents and friends and he did so with much flair and to much applause.

On the other hand, Isaac's penchant for swordplay was scary because he insisted on carrying his sword in the front of his diaper.

At first he tried inserting the sword in a cardboard scabbard draped around his neck on a string. But being at the time only a few inches taller than his sword, he kept tripping over the bottom of the scabbard or banging his knees against it. He once nearly strangled himself on the string when it snagged on a doorknob while he was running in the opposite direction from it.

Of course, Isaac wouldn't carry the sword in his hand. Heroes don't do that. He was too little for a cummerbund or whatever adult-sized thingamajig swashbucklers wore. So all I could do in the way of precaution was wince every time he thrust his flexible plastic weapon into his Pampers. I know, the sword didn't have a sharp point. And, theoretically, he couldn't hurt himself. But he did. Stabbed himself real good once, causing him to scream bloody murder and causing me to realize again how much I didn't want to become a pediatrician.

While recovering from his wound, Isaac resorted to a variety of different approaches, including carrying the sword in the back of his diaper. That sometimes wasn't the neatest place, though. He also tried letting the sword dangle from the back of his neck. That didn't work, either.

BOYHOOD SNAPSHOTS

When he walked, the tip of the sword made him lurch forward as if low-flying objects were using the backs of his knees as crash sites. Finally, he settled on inserting the sword into the back of his shirt but outside his diaper. He was safer now—but given the snafus that swords jamming into shirt labels can cause just when criminals need to be brought to justice—he was never again as quick on the draw.

It's a crying injustice to be the possessor of heroic male ambitions when you're less than three feet tall.

APPREHENSIVE SON

Dava and I took Isaac and a kindergarten girl classmate, plus Zoe and a girlfriend, to a local rodeo.

When Dava and the girls had to use a service station restroom on the way home, Isaac and I waited in the truck.

He browsed through the rodeo program until he came to a page that had a photograph of an ice cream cone.

"Is this the kind of ice cream we ate at the rodeo, Dad?" he asked.

I explained that it was an advertisement for the local ice cream company that had sponsored the bareback riding event. We talked about national brands of ice cream he knew and Isaac described different ice cream commercials he had seen.

His voice trailed off during his explanation. "I don't know about many things you know about," he said.

"It's supposed to be that way, I've lived longer," I said. "You know lots more than I knew when I was five."

He grabbed my arm. "You're going to tell me about all the things I need to know to be grown up, aren't you, Dad?"

"I'm going to try," I replied. "I won't know some of the things you want to learn about," I added, "but you'll learn them from other people or we'll put our heads together and figure them out."

"Dad, if someone calls me a chicken, I'll know what to say, right?" Isaac asked.

"Right," I said. "But you're not a chicken; you're a brave, tough kid."

"I guess I'll just tell them to stick their head in the mud," he said.

"Something like that," I said. "Everyone is afraid of something. That doesn't mean you're chicken."

DAD AND SON

"I *know* that, Dad," he said, "but sometimes I feel like I'm the only kid who is chicken. Can you tell me how to help that?"

The notion of a culture so distorted that my son had to be concerned, at age five, about being chicken, enraged me. I felt like I had nothing useful to tell him.

"Maybe we'll have to talk someday about knocking the head off the first kid who says you're a chicken," I said.

He grinned.

"But I can't stand to think that's necessary, Isaac. So let's discuss it another time, okay?"

He nodded okay and was quiet the rest of that day and evening.

DERVISH

A lot of parents take their sons to medical specialists to determine whether they're hyperactive, only to discover that the problem is both simpler and more complex than that—their sons are *male.*

Compared to other forms of humanity, *all* boys seem hyperactive.

On Father's Day, when Isaac was five, I feared he had overdosed on sugar and artificial food coloring. Here, within a ten-minute span, are the activities I had time to note:

Takes out his favorite toy of the week, a red bird whose tail you blow into to make an inner-ear-obliterating chirping sound . . . chirps into Peanuts' ear, nearly freeing his fur from his skull . . . editorializes, "Hey, Dad, did you know that Peanuts is afraid of chirping?" . . . tries to balance a toothpaste cap on his nose . . . loses the toothpaste cap under the sink . . . asks me if I brush my palms, because he saw me washing green, minty toothpaste off them, because he had coated the handle of my hairbrush with it . . . pretends he is a moose by placing beer mugs over his ears . . . swings from a stand-up lamp in my room, sending it careening into the side of the television . . . pretends he is a cat by curling up in the laundry basket . . . balances the top of a Mother's Day chocolate tin on his head . . . tries to walk while standing in the wicker cover of the kitchen trash can . . . falls onto Peanuts the Battered Cat . . . uses the bottom of the chocolate tin as a drum until Dava yells and Peanuts dashes outside . . . hooks the collar of his shirt (while wearing the shirt) over the edge of the open refrigerator door and attempts to swing from it. He and Peanuts and the rest of us somehow survive.

FRIEND

Jimmy has come over to play with Isaac. They sit shoulder touching shoulder, cross-legged, in front of the TV in the kitchen. They seem joined, each to the other. Isaac puts an arm around Jimmy, leans over and gives him a peck on the cheek, then slides away, no longer touching. Jimmy doesn't look at Isaac but slides toward him so their shoulders touch again.

At lunch, Isaac becomes upset about Jimmy drinking from a favorite mug. After a moment of Isaac crying, Jimmy says, "You know, Isaac, it doesn't matter to me what I drink from. If the mug means a lot to you, you take it." They switch mugs. Each gets the other's chocolate milk.

After lunch, they play on the back deck with a toy car wash. They discuss how sad it is they won't be able to marry each other and have children.

A month later, Jimmy and his family move away. At bedtime that night, Isaac asks me if you can take out and keep the heart of someone you love who has died.

"Not really," I reply. "You can't actually take out someone's heart and keep it because you need your heart to keep living. Are you wondering if you can keep the nice thoughts from someone's heart in your own heart?"

"Thanks, Dad, that's what I meant."

One of my best guesses ever. "Are you thinking of someone dying?"

"Yes."

"Who?"

"Guess. It's someone who used to be my best friend and moved away. Jimmy." Jimmy had been Isaac's first love outside the family. Isaac now knew despair as well as anyone.

"You think your friendship with Jimmy, the way it used to be, might be dead?"

"I'm worried about it," Isaac said.

I worried about it, too.

The next day, Isaac asked Dava to send flowers to Jimmy. A separately mailed note from Isaac, which he dictated to me, and which I sent to Jimmy, said,

---

DAD AND SON

Dear Jimmy,
Hello, I love you. Thank you for loving me.
Isaac

Jimmy's mom told us that Jimmy kept the flowers on his night table for three months.

VISIONARY

"I can't do anything for poor people," Isaac complained. "I'm too little and I can hardly read."

I said he could bring canned food to local churches to distribute to needy people in our town. He also could help kids get Christmas toys.

"Dad, do scientists ever give radio reports?" he asked.

"Yes."

"Good, when I'm a scientist someday, I'm going to give a radio report and tell the world, 'C'mon, let's really *do* something.' This world where people can starve makes me feel bad."

"You'll do good things, Isaac. And people will listen to you. They'll believe that you care."

"Dad?"

"Yes."

"That's fine, but I'm not a scientist now. What can I do now?"

"How about we send money to children like I did with Zoe a few years ago? You can do extra chores to make some of the money."

"Okay. Dad, is there anything that lasts longer than sending money or clothes or food, or giving a radio report?"

"Yes, teach people how to do things for themselves."

Isaac's eyes were bright with life. "That's it. Send them learning. If you send them learning, they won't have to keep thanking you and feeling bad about that."

I wanted to thank him. I wanted to hug and love every child in the world. I wanted to thank them for helping me to believe at moments that men might yet shape a world where people matter.

ACKNOWLEDGMENTS

The fourth and fifth chapters of the second part of this book tell you something about Gene Simons. But I want to tell you a bit more about him. He took on a job that fourteen auto body shops and van conversion centers turned down—creating what I believe is the world's first and only truck that you can drive while standing and operate entirely with hand controls. With my myopathic disorder making it impossible for me to sit or to use my legs to accelerate or brake, that's the unique vehicle I needed to get myself places. Sensing that I was broke, Gene didn't charge me for what I estimate to be more than $5,000 worth of his time. He also knowingly took incalculable legal risk—if I did any damage while driving, he could have been held responsible. Why did he do all this for me? A generous heart. I've never met a better man.

When I was too ill to type, I hired a part-time secretary who became my helping hand in every way imaginable. Ev Poitras also became my friend. Her assistance with this manuscript, from the first word of notes to the final draft, has been extraordinary. Her empathy and support have meant so much.

For his brilliance as a neurologist, his compassion as a man, and the blending of the two that it almost always takes to promote healing—my eternal thanks to John Halperin, M.D., Chairman of the North Shore Hospital Department of Neurology.

For finding a way for me to walk more than the length of a modest-size room without my Achilles tendon becoming too painful to stand on, a world of thanks to Herb Shalant, prosthetist/orthotist in Scarsdale, New York.

143

DAD AND SON

Diana Tittle was the first writer and editor to read an early draft of this book. I have gotten more encouragement, more tangible help and personal support from her over the years of writing this book than from anyone else. Her presence in my life assures me there is good in the world. She is an excellent journalist, too. And a wonderful friend.

Speaking of Diana Tittle, I can imagine her looking over my shoulder, wondering if this "acknowledgment page" is going to turn into another book. I'd better head toward home.

For their help beyond reading and commenting on my manuscript: T. Berry Brazelton, Steve Dickman, Pat Feinman, Ellen Frank, Justin Frank, Judy Grossman, Karl Horwitz, Steve Hasheider, Bill Henderson, Tom Paxton, Simon Perchik, Margery Rosen, Dava Sobel, Carey Winfrey.

For their time and support: Lee Amato, Susan Beecher, Eleanor Bergholz, Paul Bresnick, Genie Chipps, Deborah Duffy, Pam and Ron Focarino, Deb and Jeff Follenius, Max Gartenberg, Mark Grossman, Ruth Gruber, Mosa Havivi, Toby Haynes, Joni Haffner, Jeff Insler, my dad and mom—Lou and Miriam Klein, Jacqui Leader, James Levine, Peter Lisi, Millie Mascia, Bill Miller, Amy and Nick Pearson, Chiara Peacock, Honie Ann Peacock, Jimmy and Maria Preller, Ilene Rosenbaum, Susannah Ryan, Bob Sampson, Mary and Richard Shelp, Betty Sobel, Dava Sobel, Phyllis Shalant, Mark and Sandra Stollar, Philip Spitzer, Andy Torre.

I am grateful to one and all.

OF SPECIAL INTEREST

These entries are of interest to men and women concerned with equal rights and human dignity. Tortoise Books presents them as a public service. Please respond directly to the addresses shown.

AMERICAN FATHERS COALITION The federal lobbying arm of the National Congress for Fathers and Children—see below. Non-membership, all-volunteer organization. Represents 280 fathers' rights groups throughout the country. Promotes positive father-inclusive policies on a federal legislative level. Send contributions or inquiries to 2000 Pennsylvania Ave. N.W., Suite 148, Washington, D.C. 20006. Or call 1-202-FATHERS.

AT-HOME DAD A new quarterly newsletter published by Peter Baylies to provide connections and resources for the two million fathers who stay home with their children. Sections include Home Business, KidTips, Resources and At-Home Dad Network. Featured in *USA Today* and *Family Circle*. $12 per year. 61 Brightwood Ave., North Andover, MA 01845. Send SASE for more information.

THE BACKLASH Mission: Provide the information and insights needed to understand, expose and oppose anti-male bigotry, and give the men's rights community the means to network. Twenty-four-page monthly periodical focusing on the men's rights movement. $18 per year, U.S.; overseas, add $24 U.S. for postage. P.O. Box 70524, Bellevue, WA 98007-0524.

DAD-TO-DAD Founded in January, 1995, by Curtis Cooper, an at-home father from Atlanta, Georgia. Offers opportunities for at-home fathers to get together through children's play groups, dad's-night-out dinners and monthly newsletters. Two Atlanta-area chapters; working towards chapters nationwide. 120 Ashbrook Lane, Roswell, GA 30076.

FULL-TIME DADS The Magazine for Caring Fathers. Seeks to support and encourage men in their work as fathers. Offers interviews, regular feature columns, news, information, reviews and resources for and about fathers. DadsNet, a national network, helps readers start dads groups. Access to Resource File available to readers. $26 per year, U.S. (6 issues). P.O. Box 577, Cumberland, ME 04021.

HOW TO DUMP YOUR WIFE by Lee Covington. Trapped in a bad marriage? Here is straightforward, practical advice for men facing divorce. Covers all the basics: kids, lawyers, money. Includes tables listing the divorce laws in all 50 states. Be prepared! To order, call 1-800-444-2524.

MEN INTERNATIONAL A Personal and Leadership Development Organization founded in Melbourne, Australia, in 1988. Focuses solely on creating a New Leadership and a New Future for men based on their heartfelt desires, values and beliefs. Contact Robert Ware. Phone: 61+3+94995906. Fax: 61+3+94996763. E-mail: rwaremit@world.net.

M.E.N. MAGAZINE One of the few monthly publications on men's issues. Focuses on the work men are doing to understand themselves and to experience wholeness in their lives. $20 for one-year subscription. 4649 Sunnyside Ave. N., Suite 209, Seattle, WA 98103. 1-206-545-3736.

THE MEN'S DEFENSE ASSOCIATION Publishes the oldest and foremost monthly newsletter in the men's/fathers' movement. This outstanding publication, "The Liberator," deals with a wide range of gender issues from the male viewpoint—primarily divorce, employment, crime/punishment and image. Writers include prominent attorneys, educators and sociologists. $24 per year. 17854 Lyons St., Forest Lake, MN 55025.

THE MEN'S INTERNETWORK (TMI) An ad hoc, virtual community of men's rights activists. Please join and push for gender equity via cyberspace. No dues or forms to sign. Just contact Robert Sides (first male alum of Radcliffe's Graduate Program in Management!) at "JoinTMI@aol.com." Or write to TMI, P.O. Box 15311, Kenmore Station, Boston, MA 02115.

THE NATIONAL CENTER FOR MEN Supports total gender equality. Emphasizes equal rights and equal responsibilities; prosecuting perjury; business skills rather than government intervention; shared parenting, reward cooperation and enforced visitation. "Activism first, report second." Headquarters: P.O. Box 555, Old Bethpage, NY 11804, 1-516-942-2020. West Coast: P.O. Box 6481, Portland, OR 97228-6481, 1-503-727-3686.

THE NATIONAL COALITION OF FREE MEN One of the oldest men's rights groups. Believes in equal access to opportunity and equal imposition of responsibilities for both sexes. Dues are $30 per year ($40 foreign). Includes a subscription to "Transitions," the bimonthly Journal of Men's Perspectives, which examines gender issues from the masculist point of view. P.O. Box 149, Manhasset, NY 11030. 1-516-482-6378.

NATIONAL CONGRESS FOR FATHERS AND CHILDREN Encourages with a single nationwide voice the vital role of fathers in the growth and development of their children. Supports fathers' rights, men's rights and divorce reform in North America. "The Best Parent Is Both Parents." $60 for annual membership, including quarterly newsletter and divorce information manual. P.O. Box 171675, Kansas City, KS 66117-1675. 1-800-SEE-DADS.

POETRY "Letters to the Dead" by Simon Perchik. Perchik's poems have appeared in *Partisan Review, The New Yorker* and dozens of other noted publications. "His poetry is abstract, but poignantly and powerfully clear with images that enhance our understanding, our dignity and our humanness"—Art Klein. $8.95 plus $2.50 shipping. Simon Perchik, 10 Whitby Lane, East Hampton, NY 11937.

SINGLE PARENTING IN THE NINETIES Newsletter published for single parents. Written mostly by readers to provide a monthly guide where single parents can learn from one another. Also features quotes from children in single-parent families to help parents understand their views. Write for details. 6910 W. Brown Deer Road, Suite 269-A, Milwaukee, WI 53223-2104.

T-SHIRTS (1) "Good Fathers Are Good Men"—L and XL; black and red on white. (2) Real Men Can Love—M, L, XL; black on white. 100% good-quality cotton, not preshrunk. $10 plus $2 shipping, $1 more for each extra shirt. Male Redefined, P.O. Box 3142, East Hampton, NY 11937.

AUDIOTAPES by James Sniechowski, Ph.D and Judith Sherven, Ph.D. $10 each, plus $2 shipping for one tape, 75 cents extra for each additional. Small Kindnesses Press, 12021 Wilshire Blvd., Suite 692, Los Angeles, CA 90025.

"Breaking Through Resistance" (Sherven)—Learn to identify the Inner Saboteur that blocks you from living fully.

"Calling Men to Community" (Sniechowski)—Enhancing men's capacity for intimacy and their sense of place in the world.

"Embracing Intimacy" (Sniechowski and Sherven)—Probing beliefs and expectations of intimate relationships, and opening more fully to loving partnership.

"Fathering the Boy Within" (Sniechowski)—Discovering, understanding and changing the way men express their maleness.

"Mothering the Girl Within" (Sherven)—Helps women examine how and what they learned about being women.

"Reclaiming the Self" (Sherven and Sniechowski)—This 10-tape series is ideal for independent use and as an adjunct to counseling, psychotherapy and 12-step recovery work. Includes: "Breaking Through Resistance" . . . "You Are the Healer" . . . "Embracing Intimacy" . . . "Mothering the Girl Within" . . . "Womanhood: Power and Identity" . . . "Calling Men to Community" . . . "Fathering the Boy Within" . . . and the "Sons and Fathers" 3-tape series.

"Sons and Fathers" (Sniechowski)—Healing the distance between son and father. Three tapes: "To Explore Our Wounds," "To Heal Our Wounds," "To Forgive Ourselves."

ORDER AND REFERRAL FORM

Please photocopy this page to order additional copies of *Dad and Son*—or to have us send free information to your friend(s).

Yes, please send me:

QUANTITY

_____ *Dad and Son: A Memoir About Reclaiming Fatherhood and Manhood*, by Art Klein. $20 hardcover. Plus $3.50 shipping and handling for one copy, $1 more for each additional copy. New York residents add the applicable state sales tax.

_____ *Dad and Son: A Memoir About Reclaiming Fatherhood and Manhood*, by Art Klein. $12.95 softcover. Plus $3 shipping and handling for one copy, $.75 more for each additional copy. New York residents add the applicable state sales tax.

Special rates available for men's organizations; contact Tortoise Books at the address below.

☐ Payment enclosed

☐ Please charge my _____Visa _____ MasterCard

Account # _____

Expiration Date _____

Signature _____

Name _____

Address _____

City _____ State _____ Zip _____

☐ Check here to get a free bumper sticker, "Good Fathers Are Good Men"

☐ Please send free information about *Dad and Son* to:

Name _____

Address _____

City _____ State _____ Zip _____

Name _____

Address _____

City _____ State _____ Zip _____

Mail form to: Tortoise Books
               191 Harbor Watch Court
               Sag Harbor, New York 11963

Or call/fax: 516-725-9465